Francis Bacon

培根论说文集
Essays

弗兰西斯·培根　　著

外语教学与研究出版社

FOREIGN LANGUAGE TEACHING AND RESEARCH PRESS

北京　BEIJING

京权图字 01－97－1104

图书在版编目(CIP)数据

培根论说文集:英文/(英)培根(Bacon,F.)著.— 北京:外语教学与研究出版社,1997.9 (2007.11 重印)
(大师经典文库)
ISBN 978－7－5600－1360－2

Ⅰ.论…　Ⅱ.培…　Ⅲ.英语—语言读物　Ⅳ.H319.4:B

中国版本图书馆 CIP 数据核字 (97) 第 24285 号

出 版 人：于春迟
责任编辑：李　程
出版发行：外语教学与研究出版社
社　　址：北京市西三环北路 19 号 (100089)
网　　址：http://www.fltrp.com
印　　刷：北京一二零一印刷厂
开　　本：850×1168　1/32
印　　张：6.125
版　　次：1998 年 4 月第 1 版　2007 年 11 月第 8 次印刷
书　　号：ISBN 978－7－5600－1360－2
定　　价：6.90 元
＊　　＊　　＊

The paper in this book is produced from pure wood
pulp,without the use of chlorine or any other substance
harmful to the environment.The energy used in its
production consists almost entirely of hydroelectricity
and heat generated from waste material,thereby
conserving fossil fuels and contributing little
to the greenhouse effect

This edition published 1997 byWordsworth Editions Limited
Cumberland House,Crib Street,Ware,Hertfordshire SG12 9ET

ISBN 1 85326 472 5

Typeset in Great Britain by Antony Gray
Printed and bound in Denmark by Nørhaven

出版说明

　　我社自90年代以来，一直以促进国际文化交流为己任，致力于原版外语著作的引进和出版工作，逐步形成了规模化、系列化、精品化的出版传统，在广大读者中产生了一定的影响。但是，目前我国外语图书出版呈现出较为严重的不均衡局面，即文艺类图书品种相对齐全，而人文科学、社会科学类外语图书的出版却寥寥可数，远远滞后于日益增长的文化市场需求。为了填补这一空白，我社编辑出版了这套英文版哲学、社会科学类丛书"大师经典文库"，系统地推出一批世界著名思想家、哲学家、历史学家、心理学家的经典学术名著，包括我国古代哲学籍典的权威英译本，为广大英语学习者提供高质量的阅读文本，也为各类社会科学研究工作者提供必备的学术资料。本丛书每一种均由著名专家、学者撰写评介性的序言。

外语教学与研究出版社
1997 年 11 月

序　言

程孟辉

　　弗兰西斯·培根 (Francis Bacon, 1561－1626) 是17世纪英国的著名思想家、政治家和经验主义哲学家，同时又是实验科学的前驱者，出身于伦敦一个新贵族家庭，其父尼可拉斯·培根爵士是伊丽莎白女王的掌玺大臣。因而，培根是在一种充满着政治国事氛围的家庭环境中成长起来的，这无疑对他的一生影响极大。培根12岁 (1573年) 进入剑桥大学三一学院读书，在校期间，对当时被教会奉为经典的经院哲学深为不满，认为它流于空论，对人生无实际效益。1576年受命赴巴黎，出任英国驻法国大使随员，1579年因父丧回国，后于1582年转而从事律师工作，并当选为国会议员，1596年被女王聘为特别法律顾问，1607年任副检察长，六年后，晋升为总检察长，1617年转任掌玺大臣，1618年被加封为大法官兼上议院议长。培根一生曾多次接受王室的封号，1603年受封为爵士，1618年受封为维露廉男爵，1620年受封为圣阿尔班子爵。1621年因被控受贿(培根本人对此亦供认不讳) 而被免去官职，另被判处罚金四万镑，监禁于伦敦塔中，期限随国王的旨意而定，终生逐出朝廷，不准再任官职。不过，这个判决实际只执行了一小部分，也没有强令其缴付罚款。培根本人在伦敦塔内只被监禁了四天。由于被免官革职，重进官场无望，故转而从事学术研究和撰述著作，聊度余年。五年后 (即1626年)，培根因在一次关于雪的防腐作用的野外试验中遭受风寒而病逝，终年65岁。

在培根65年的一生中，尽管他大半时间混迹于官场，但他与许多官僚政客不同的是，他始终矢志于推进人类知识与文明的发展。培根的一生著述颇丰，且涉及的领域广泛，其中包括政治、经济、哲学、历史、法律、宗教、艺术、教育、科学、婚姻与道德、社交与休闲、民风与习俗等等。1597年，《培根论说文集》问世，这是一本关于政治伦理道德艺术论等方面的文集，出版后，在当时产生了不小的影响，并又分别于1612、1625年两次增订再版。培根企图将全部的科学、技术和人类的一切知识进行全面的改造和重建，故而他倾全力撰述宏篇巨著《伟大的复兴》，尽管此项工程未能全部完成(只完成了第一、第二两部，即《学术的进展》〔1625〕和《新工具》〔1620〕)，但它对西方乃至整个人类思想产生了巨大而又深远的影响。除此之外，培根还撰述了专门研究古代文化的学术论著《论古人的智慧》(1609)，此书通过古代希腊神话表述了培根对政治、科学和哲学等问题的见解。此外，法律和历史方面的著作有《亨利第七朝史》(1622)，幻想游记方面的有《新大西岛》(1626)等。

培根，作为人类思想史上的一个重要人物，作为一个伟大的思想家，他具有一种与众不同的历史地位。当人们对培根进行全面思考时，便会自然而然地提出这样的问题：培根一生，写过重要的哲学著作，但在他的哲学著作中，关注的并非那些为人们所公认的纯哲学问题，因此，也有一些人就此认为，培根难以望近代哲学史上一流的哲学家项背，还有人认为，培根尽管对科学研究有执著的追求，甚至可以说，他几乎把毕生的精力贡献给了科学研究事业，然而，他终究算不上真正意义上的科学家。再拿教育来说，培根一生从未当过教员，他也没有从事过任何真正的教育实践，然而，西方的一些教育家们却认为"他对教育思想所产生的影响比任何或全部教育家的影响更大"。① 培根没有专门的经济学著作，然而，令人不可思议的是，他的大名却常常出现在

① 博伊德等著：《西方教育史》，人民教育出版社1985年版，第233页。

经济思想史一类的著作中。此外，培根没有专门的美学专著，但美学史家们屡屡在其史著中怀着由衷的敬仰之情予以歌颂和礼赞，如此等等。这种学术研究史上的种种奇特现象说明了什么？的确，无论是纵向地或者是横向地看培根，我们认为，在任何一个具体的学术领域，人们都很难说培根是第一流的人物，然而，就人类文明发展的整个历史长河而言，培根乃是当之无愧的第一流的思想家。早在19世纪的德国，古典哲学的集大成者黑格尔就对培根作了如是评说：尽管此人不喜欢抽象的推理，但他终究是经验主义的奠基人。[①] 英国现代分析哲学家罗素在谈到培根哲学的历史功绩和地位时，一方面承认他的哲学有许多不尽人意或不够完善的地方，但另一方面又认为，不管怎么说，就其哲学的价值而言，培根"仍旧占有永远不倒的地位"。[②] 无论是19世纪的德国哲学家黑格尔，还是20世纪的现代英国大哲罗素，他们都从不同的角度看到了培根思想的特征和价值。

培根思想的最大贡献莫过于科学和哲学方面，就其思想的价值和历史地位而言，革命导师马克思对之曾作过精确的评价，称他是"英国唯物主义和整个现代实验科学的真正始祖"。[③] 培根反对经院哲学和唯心主义，提出"假相"说，认为经院哲学使人与自然隔绝，束缚于教条和权威之下，不能获得真正的知识。他主张打破"假相"，消除各种幻想和偏见。他还主张"双重真理说"，强调发展自然科学的重要性，提出知识就是力量，认为掌握知识的目的是认识自然，以便征服自然。他指出，自然界不是精神，而是物质的东西，而这物质是多种多样的，能动的，具有内在的力量和强力，一切知识都来源于感觉，感觉才是唯一真实

---

① 参见黑格尔：《哲学史讲演录》第四卷，商务印书馆1983年版，第31页。

② 参见罗素：《西方哲学史》下卷，商务印书馆1976年版，第61页。

③ 《马克思恩格斯全集》第二卷，人民出版社，第163页。

5

可靠的。科学在整理感性材料时，用的是归纳、分析、比较、观察和实验的理性方法等等。培根思想的进步性反映了英国资产阶级上升时期对发展科学的合理要求，但其学说中也犹如马克思所指出的那样，充满了"神学的不彻底性"，如认为有不死的"理性灵魂"的存在。在教育方面，他强调学校应该传授百科全书式的知识，在美学方面，培根从其科学的实践观点和归纳方法出发，将美学由玄学思辨的领域转到科学的领域，从而使由他的思想发展出来的英国经验派美学朝着科学的方向前进。下面，我们就沿着上述培根思想的轨迹作一概述。

综观培根的整个哲学思想，我们认为，知识论始终是其核心。培根一直把改造人类的知识、实现科学的"伟大的复兴"、建立一个能促进生产发展和技术进步的新哲学当作自己理论活动的目的。培根对人类的心智能力始终是寄予信心和厚望的。他看到了人的智慧和认识能力所蕴含的巨大力量和价值，认为只要人们认识到自己的这种力量，并将这种力量付诸实践性的尝试，那么，人类将会获得更多更有价值的东西。就拿人和自然的关系来说，一方面，人是自然的仆役，人在自然面前必须服从其规律，遵循其法则，另一方面，人可以发现和掌握自然的规律，找到自然的法则，人在发现自然、认识自然的过程中，逐步地可以征服自然，改造自然，驾驭自然，成为自然的主人。培根在人与自然的关系问题上，已经悟到了二者之间的辩证关系，即一方面自然法则不可违背，另一方面，人对自然的认识是人征服、改造、驾驭自然的前提条件。由此，培根得出结论认为：人要命令自然，就要服从自然，而人类命令、驾驭、征服自然的力量源泉在于对自然规律或自然法则的认识，而知识就是对规律或法则的认识。在培根之前不久由意大利航海家哥伦布完成的地理大发现给他以深刻的印象和启示。培根认为，中国印刷术、火药和指南针的发现和发明"改变了全世界的整个面貌和事态"，尤其使培根感到欣喜和鼓舞的是哥伦布的地理大发现和伽利略用天文望远镜所揭示的宇宙新景象，因为，这是人类用其新的知识力量发现的征服自然的最好标志和典范。当代英国著名学者、伦敦大学教授亚·沃尔夫在谈到上述科学启示时这样写道："培根还想亲自作出实用的发明，并发现一个新世界，至少是一个'新的理智的世界'。为此，他提议找出当代学者的缺陷，详细制订关于协同研究的新方法的计划，这些新方法能够导致真正的知识和实用的结果。他为履行这个计划所做的主要贡献包括在他的《学术的进展》(Advancement of Learning)、《新工具》(Novum Organum)和《新大西岛》(New Atlantis)之中。值得指出的是，这些著作中最重要的一部《新工具》的扉页上是一幅图，一艘张满帆的船驶过旧世界的尽头'海格立斯柱'而进入大西洋去探寻新世界。培根显然志在成为'新的理智世界的'哥伦布。"① 的确，沃尔夫的上述论断是对培根作为思想家的恰如其分的评价。培根的一生，犹如哥伦布一样，在人类知识的海洋上勇敢地探险，为了寻找一个"新的理智世界"，他付出的实在是太多了。

培根重视科学知识，倡导科学探索，并不是为了科学本身，而是为了利用科学知识，并把它作为一种为人类谋求福利的有效手段（或工具）。培根深知，在他那个时代（16、17世纪），广大的人民还生活在粗野而又悲惨的境况中，迫切需要某种力量去解救。生活在贫困线上的饥寒交迫的人们，由于他们在现世中得不到幸福、舒适和快慰，故自然而然地对现实产生绝望，而把渴望过幸福生活的理想寄予来世或彼岸。在贫困的人群中，人们普遍乞求神灵、魔法和占星术，加之传统上对奇迹的迷信和流行的神秘的泛灵论的自然观助长了对占星术、魔法和巫术的信仰，因

---

① 亚·沃尔夫：《十六、十七世纪科学、技术和哲学史》，商务印书馆1985年版，第708页。

此，即便是像卜勒刻这样的伟大天文学家，也免不了是个神秘主义者和占星士。培根面对这种实际生活中的现象，他坚持认为，驾驭自然的唯一途径是利用科学知识而不是巫术的或占星术的仪式。神秘主义的操作 (这里主要是指巫术或占星术等) 不可能制服自然现象。对于自然现象，人们应予以研究、遵守、服从。只有理解它们的特征和规律，它们才有可能被用来造福于人类。由此可见，培根关于"对自然的知识"的思想是服从于实践目的的，并且他一直为实现这一实践目的而不懈地努力。在培根看来，一切人类知识的最后的也是唯一的任务就是利用人类对世界的认识来征服全世界。培根提出了"知识就是力量"的著名论断。在他看来，知识不但就是力量，而且是唯一持久的力量。德国哲学史家文德尔班就此指出："如果说魔术利用奇异的艺技力图主宰自然，那么，此种盲目的企图在培根那里变得明朗起来，并得到了这样的认识：人类之所以能支配事物，只是由于对事物的真正本质作过理智的调查研究。人只有服从〔自然〕才能统治〔自然〕。因此，对他说来，解释自然只不过是人类理智克服自然的手段。"① 人类理智水平如何，取决于人类的知识程度。那么，人类又如何能够获得真正的而且又富有成果的知识呢? 换言之，人类是通过什么方式或手段获得征服自然的知识的呢? 对此，培根作出了如是回答，即摆脱成见和采取正确的探索方法。关于摆脱成见，培根坚持认为，一切科学知识都必须从不带偏见的观察开始。然而，在实践中要真正做到这一点是十分不易的，因为，人的心灵犹如一面魔镜，它反映某种虚假的或失真的映像，这种虚假的或失真的映像是由于某种缠绕于人的心灵的成见或"假相"所致。培根将这些假相分别称之为"种族假相"、"洞穴假相"、"市场假相"和"剧场假相"，并对这四种假相分别

---

① 文德尔班:《哲学史教程》下卷，商务印书馆1993年版，第530页。

作了分析和批判 (关于这四种"假相", 下文将另有细述)。关于采取正确的探索方法, 这是培根强调的又一要点, 因为它是获得科学知识所必须的基本条件。在这一点上, 培根主张应该把经验主义和理性主义、仔细的观察和正确的推理结合起来, 并且, 他用一种比喻的方式生动形象地把单纯的经验主义者比作蚂蚁, 把单纯的理性主义者比作蜘蛛, 认为经验主义者 (或曰实验家)之所以像蚂蚁, 是因为他们只知道采集和利用, 理性主义者 (或曰推理家) 之所以像蜘蛛, 是因为他们只知用自己的物质编织蜘蛛网, 唯独科学家不但像蚂蚁那样会采集原料, 而且用自己的力量来变革和处理这些原料。因此, 培根认为, 科学家是知识的象征, 力量的象征。科学家之所以为科学家, 就是因为他掌握了科学。要促进科学的发展, 必须要有正确的理论和方法指导, 因而培根着重研究了认识论和方法论的问题。正是这些研究, 使培根成为近代经验主义认识论的创始人和科学归纳法的奠基者。

培根的经验主义认识论是在反对经院哲学的斗争中确立起来的。培根认为, 一切观念和知识都起源于感觉经验, 经验乃是一切知识的源泉, 人们若要想获得真正的知识, 就必须把认识建立在经验及其科学实验的基础上。相反, 经院哲学脱离实际, 玩弄概念, 崇尚空谈。经院哲学家的玄学思辨不解决任何实际问题, 它犹如蜘蛛那样, 只会从自己腹中吐出丝来织网, 而真正的哲学家就应该像蜜蜂那样, 从各种花蕊中采得甜汁, 然后通过自己的消化, 把它转化为蜜。这也就是说, 哲学家不应从概念出发, 而应从感性经验出发。然而, 培根同时也承认, 纯粹地凭感性也不行, 因为人的感官往往是带有欺骗性的。在人们的头脑中, 往往带有不同程度的种种迷信思想或偏见, 所以将这些迷信或偏见归纳起来, 培根提出了著名的四种"假相" (idole) 说, 这就是上文提及的"种族假相" (idola tribus)、"洞穴假相" (idola specus)、"市场假相"(idola fori)和"剧场假相"(idola theatri)。培根认为，所谓的"种族假相"是指整个种族(或人类)所共有的成见，例如，它倾向于只看到并相信为人们所赞同的东西，在万物中看到一种目的，用拟人的方法解释一切，使自己成为衡量外在世界的尺度，盲目地保留由印象所引起的思想模式；"洞穴假相"就是指每个个体的人被他的天性和生活环境禁锢于他的"洞穴"之中，从而产生一种偏爱等特有的个人成见。培根以与他同时代的吉尔伯特博士为例，此人"在极其勤奋地从事磁石的研究和观察之后，立刻就着手按照他所偏爱的这个问题构造一个完整的哲学体系"；①"市场假相"，这类错误主要来自于人与人之间的互相交流，尤其是语言交流。因为人们往往用语言或语词代替概念。例如，人们一般都倾向于认为，同他们所使用的一切名称相对应的事物是存在的，例如机遇、命运、巫术等等，也倾向于忽略一个语词的字面意义和隐喻意义的差别(例如有限与无限在应用于物理和非物理客体时的那种情况)。培根把这些情形归因于这样的事实：　"学者们激烈而严肃的争执往往终止于围绕着词和名称的论争"；②"剧场假相"则是指人们轻信历史上的理论而又不经过自己独立思索和判断、人云亦云的虚妄观念，它是特别忠于特定的哲学、神学体系的产物。培根认为，"一切公认的［哲学］体系都只不过是许多舞台上的戏剧，按照一种不真实的布景方式来表现它们自己所创造的世界罢了。"，③

亚里士多德、毕达哥拉斯，还有那些近代人，"他们试图根据《创世记》前几章或《约伯记》和圣书的其他部分来建立一种自然哲学

①②③　参见亚·沃尔夫：《十六、十七世纪科学、技术和哲学史》，商务印书馆1985年版，第711页。

体系。"，① 培根之所以要详细论述以上四种假相，旨在阐明这四种存在于人们头脑中的由来已久的假相是人们正确认识自然的大敌，是科学 (发展) 的大敌。培根正是通过对上述四种假相的剖析，抨击经院哲学只知道玩弄词句，搞概念游戏，抨击腐朽权威的统治，抨击经院哲学所鼓吹的神人同性学说，从而提出要亲自检验事物本身，不要人云亦云，要不带任何偏见地去接受现实。总之，他要求科学家和一切与科学有关的人们，如果要想获得使人类驾驭物质世界的知识，从而进入建基于科学之上的王国，那么，他就必须从其心灵中清除所有上述四种"假相"。

在崇尚科学的道路上，培根不但对四种"假相"作了分析批判，同时，他还对亚里士多德的逻辑三段论予以根本性的否定。培根否定亚里士多德逻辑三段论的主要理由是：它由命题所组成，命题是由语词所组成，而语词则代表概念。如果概念混乱，即是由粗率的事物抽绎而成 (实际情形正是这样)，那么，整个上层建筑就不牢固。三段论中的概念、原则和公理都建立在模糊和错误的经验基础上，这其实是对经验的轻率概括。因此，它不能发现科学原理，旧的归纳法 (即简单枚举法) 得不出可靠的结论。培根认为，必须要清除科学之路上的种种障碍，制订出认识自然的新工具和新方法。在《新工具》一书中，培根提出要建立一种新的逻辑体系，这个新的逻辑体系就是区别于亚里士多德逻辑三段论的"归纳法"。他认为，唯有归纳法才是处理事实的最正确的方法。人们在对自己的观察和探究中，他们借助于归纳法就有可能获得一般的认识 (或公理)，从而可以最后达到据此解释其他现象的目的。培根强调观察和实验，不主张那种从经验材料直接飞跃到最普遍公理的认识方法。在培根看来，从感性上升

---

① 亚·沃尔夫：《十六、十七世纪科学技术和哲学史》，商务印书馆1985年版，第711页。

到理性的过程不是一个跳跃式的突变过程，而是呈逐渐递升的过程。这是培根归纳法的一个基本原则。这一原则是对当时自然科学中的实验分析方法的总结，它对当时自然科学的发展起了很大的推动作用。同时，它在反对经院哲学的空洞烦琐的演绎推理方面亦起了积极的作用。但是，培根片面地夸大归纳法，贬低演绎法，不理解分析与综合的辩证关系，便形成了形而上学的思维方式。

作为唯物主义哲学家，培根在对世界的看法上始终坚持其唯物主义的自然观。例如，他认为世界是物质的，在自然界中，真实存在的是无数个体事物，构成物体的最基本成分是"简单性质"，这些性质的数目很多，然而都是有限不变的。一切事物中都存在着"形式"，即"潜伏的结构"和"潜伏的过程"（或曰"事物内部的规律"）。形式和简单结构的关系是本质和现象、原因和结果的关系。培根不主张把物质视为抽象的东西，相反，他认为，运动是物质自身所固有的特征。运动是绝对的，静止是相对的。静止是由物质运动的均衡或由物质运动的绝对优势所引起的。在物体表面的静止中，物体内部的物质分子仍在不停地运动着。培根还强调指出物质的无限性和永久存在性，物质并不是由什么东西产生而被什么东西所消灭，没有什么东西比物质更原始的了。物质是原因之原因。因此，培根主张，无论是研究物质也好，还是研究自然规律也好，都必须要研究其"简单的性质"，从中去发现它的"形式"，人们一旦发现了形式，在思想方面能得到真理，在实践方面就能得到自由。当然，人们在研究物质时，最关键的是要抓住物质的"运动"性质，因为运动乃是物质的第一重要的特性。

从培根的唯物主义自然观中，我们可以看到，其中不乏辩证的思想因素，它与后来的机械唯物主义有很大的不同。不过，由于时代和阶级的局限，培根的唯物主义也是不彻底的，例如他把上帝说成是万物的最高主宰，承认"双重真理"，从而表现出他对神学批判的不彻底性。

培根除了对科学、哲学的贡献外，我们在这里再值得书上一笔的是他在美学上的贡献。培根一生，尽管他把主要精力用在"科学的复兴"上，但对美学问题也曾给予了相当的关注。培根本人虽然没有撰写过专门的美学论著，但在《培根论说文集》的58篇论说文中，一篇《论美》文章，深刻地表达了培根对美的精深见解，加之，还有其他的几篇，如《论建筑》、《论花园》、《论宫剧与盛会》和《论礼节与仪容》等文章，都从各个不同的角度折射出培根的美学思想。因此，如果一部美学思想史竟然不提及培根，这不能不说是该著的一种缺憾。值得指出的是，培根的经验主义哲学观点，对其美学思想产生了很大的影响。在培根的诸多美学观点中，最重要的一点是：他认为"美的精华在于文雅的动作"。在《论美》中，培根这样写道："在美方面，相貌的美高于色泽的美，而秀雅合式的动作美又高于相貌的美。这是美的精华，是绘画所表现不出来的，对生命的第一眼印象也是如此，没有哪一种高度的美不在比例上出现几分奇特。很难断定在亚帕利斯① 和杜勒② 两位画家之中的哪一位比较肤浅，杜勒要按照几何比例去画人像，而亚帕利斯却从许多面孔中选择最好的部分去画一个最美的面孔。我并非说这两种画像不能叫任何人满意，除掉画家自己。我并非说画家不应该把面孔画得比实际的更美，我只是说他在画的时候，应该凭一种得心应手的轻巧(就像音乐家奏出一个优美的曲调那样)，而不是凭死规矩。我们常

---

①② 亚帕利斯是公元前4世纪的希腊大画家，曾替亚历山大画过像，他在训练上特别看重素描。杜勒(公元1471－1528)是德国大画家，曾留学意大利。文艺复兴时期意大利的艺术大师，多半强调比例的研究，杜勒受此影响，著有《论比例》一书。

看到一些面孔，就其中各部分孤立地看，看不出丝毫的优点，但是就整体看，它们都显得很美，如果美的精华在于高雅的动作这句话不错，老年人比青年人往往美得多这个事实就当然不足为奇了。拉丁谚语说得好：'秋天的美才是真正的美。'因为只有带着宽容的意味，并且承认青年人的美是由于他们年轻，才可以说青年人美。美就像夏天的果子，容易烂，留不住。就大多数情形来说，青年人美，就容易放荡，到老来，就失去恩宠。但是另一方面，如果美碰巧落在一个正当的人身上，也就一定会使他的德行放射出光辉，使他的罪过引起面孔上羞惭的红晕。"① 从培根的上述论断中，我们看到，他重视对人的美的研究，而人的美无疑包含着以下两个方面的内容：一是人的形体相貌（外在）的美，二是人的精神品格（内在）的美。前者是指人的物质美范畴，后者则是指人的精神美范畴。突出重视和研究人(包括人体)的美，这是自文艺复兴以来的一大时代特征。无论是思想家还是艺术家们都普遍相信人的智慧和力量，要求一切以人为本。美的东西也只有在人那里得到最完满的体现。如果我们说：一幢建筑很美，一片彩霞很美，一座山峰很美，这种人为之美或自然之美，都只是一种纯粹的物质性美，因为无论是建筑物，还是彩霞和山峰，它们都是无生命、无灵魂的东西，而人则不同，他除了由物质构成的躯体外，还包含有思想和灵魂（或曰精神）。因此，任何人的美都有其内在美和外在美（即精神美和物质美）的双重衡量尺度。一个外在很美而道德品格不好或知识欠缺，或举止粗卑的人，就很难说他是美的。这里，精神的因素起了很大的作用。这正如黑格尔所言的那样："人的躯体不是一种单纯的自然存在，而是在形状和构造上既表示它是精神的感性的自然存

---

① 培根：《论美》(朱光潜译文)，转引自：《西文美学家论美和美感》，商务印书馆1981年版，第77－78页。

在，又表现出一种更高的内在生活，因此就不同于动物的躯体，尽管它和动物的躯体大体上很一致。"① 因此，培根认为，在一个人的身体上，很难做到既有外在美，又具内在美。有些科学家或具有高超技艺的人尽管他们的长相挺美，但缺乏远大的志向，不注重道德修养，这样的人是称不起美的。当然，这也不是绝对的，培根认为，品貌双全的美人也是有的，但毕竟不具有普遍性。培根关于人的美的论点，其主旨是强调人的内在精神之美，与人的外在美相比，内在之美才是真正的美的精华。人体的外貌之美犹如夏日的水果，随着时间的推延而终究要"衰退"，而唯独精神美可以永葆青春、永垂不衰。由此，培根提出了青年人和老年人各有不同之美的审美标准，老年人可以由于丰富的知识和高深的修养等因素而给人一种德高望重的成熟之美，真可谓越老越美越可爱。培根美学思想的最高境界是美德与美貌的和谐结合。除了关于人的美的论点外，培根在其《培根论说文集》中还就造型艺术、诗歌艺术和宫廷戏剧等提出了自己的独特看法。对于培根的美学贡献，我们也应该从他的科学观点和科学方法角度去认识。正是由于培根奠定了科学实践观点和归纳方法的基础，才使其美学有可能从玄学思辨的领域转到科学的领域。应该看到，培根的美学思想对英国经验派美学产生了巨大而又深远的影响。

关于培根的生平、成就、学术思想及其历史地位，暂且叙述到这里，至于《培根论说文集》一书，鉴于奥利芬特·斯韦顿先生为该书写了一篇世所公认的定评性绪论，故本文就不再对此详作细论了。不过，尽管如此，我仍有必要就此书的有关问题向读者作以下叙述：

---

① 黑格尔：《美学》第三卷（上册），商务印书馆1979年版，第126—127页。

第一，《培根论说文集》共收论文58篇。就这些论文所涉的内容而言，概括起来可分为以下三类，即人与世界及人群的关系；人与自身的关系；人与上帝的关系。这些文章不仅对创立英国文学新风起了重大作用，而且对近代唯物主义哲学及科学的思想方法也有很大的影响。

第二，《培根论说文集》不是一部一气呵成的著作，而是一部经作者多年反复锤炼、推敲、修改而成的精工之作。凡是细细阅读过该书的人，都不难看出，它是作者自己的经历之谈，是培根毕生的经验总结。从那58篇论文的字里行间，人们可以看出作者的智慧和独具匠心。用斯韦顿先生的话来说："凡是细心研究过他的这些文章的人，没有一个不发现它们是作者自己的经验之结果，而经过他的奇妙的心智所陶冶锻炼过的。没有一篇文章里面不包含着一两句话，把那篇文章的主旨或结论与作者的生平关联起来。这种关联有时微妙不显，有时却很明显。培根的《论说文集》可说是少数的'世界书'的一部，这种书不是为一国而作，乃是为万国而作的，不是为一个时代，而是为一切时代的。在这本书里，极高的智力与变化无穷的兴趣和同情心合而为一了，所以，世人之中，无论什么样的类型或脾气，都可以在这部书里找到一点与他有联系的东西。在培根的时代，颇有几本专门描写刻画英国人的性格、地方人士和习俗的书……培根要写这样的书是很容易的。但是，假如他真的这样写了，那就只有英国人能充分领略书中的精神和情绪了。而现在培根的《论说文集》的影响可说是仅为世界的四极所限，因为既然大家都能懂，自然无人不能享受了。"[1] 总之，文字精练、内容丰富、贴近生活、雅俗共赏是《培根论说文集》的一大特点。

---

[1] 《培根论说文集》，商务印书馆1958年版，第5页。

第三，《培根论说文集》的成书过程大致经历了三个阶段，这三个阶段的标志分别为：1597、1612和1625年出版的三个不同版本。第一版出版于1597年，当时只有10篇文章，也许是由于显得太单薄了，故又增补了一篇《宗教默想》（Religious Meditations）。到了1612年出版时，已由原来的10篇增加到38篇。而且原先的10篇文章也多半作了较大的修改，甚至有的篇章几乎是重新撰写的。从那时起到培根逝世时止的那一版，即末版，共收文章58篇。自第一版成书后，作者前后28年一直将此书随时携带于身，不断地加以增删、修改，故此书随着培根个人阅历的丰富和知识的增长而不断地得以修改、充实和完善，如该文集中的《论请托》、《论党派》和《论友谊》等文章，各个不同的版本都有重大的修改。由此可见作者对此书的用心之良苦。

第四，综观《培根论说文集》中的58篇论文，涉及到人生世事的方方面面，几乎人们在日常生活中所遇到的，其中也都有所论及。看看那些《论真理》、《论死亡》、《论高位》、《论嫉妒》、《论恋爱》、《论迷信》、《论野心》、《论虚荣》……等文章，我们不难看到，作者一生始终希冀用知识的眼光和经验主义的认识论去思考人生，探究世界。尽管他的思想观点由于受历史的局限而难免在我们今人看来失之偏颇，但这不应该成为影响我们对培根作出客观评价的理由。当然，要对培根这样的思想家作评价的确不是一件容易的事，还是韦斯顿先生说得好："就智力方面说，培根是伟大的；就道德方面说，他是很弱的。他的人格是多方面的，他的天才不限于一隅。他是法学家、政客、科学家、哲学家、历史学家，又是散文作家。对于这样繁复的性格与才能要下一个总评是很难的。"①斯韦顿先生的上述论点，也许可以给我们以这样的启示：每一个手捧《培根论说文集》的读

---

① 《培根论说文集》，商务印书馆1958年版，第20页。

者，当你从这位先人的智慧和思想光芒中领略到什么时，你就可以根据你对这位先哲的了解所达到的知晓程度，得出一种结论。怎么评价，全由你自己了。因为，除了你自己，别人不会勉强你，更不会武断地指责你。就我个人而言，结论性的评价当然是：培根，作为人类的思想家，他是伟大的，不朽的。同样，作为他思想的一个缩影，《培根论说文集》也将永远在人类的思想宝库中闪闪发光，与世长存。

CONTENTS

CONTENTS

CONTENTS

FRANCIS BACON
ESSAYS

To the Right Honourable
my very good lord
the Duke of Buckingham
his Grace,
Lord High Admiral of England

EXCELLENT LORD – Solomon says; a good name is as a precious ointment; and I assure my self, such will your Grace's name be, with posterity. For your fortune, and merit both, have been eminent. And you have planted things, that are like to last. I do now publish my essays; which, of all my other works, have been most current: for that, as it seems, they come home, to men's business, and bosoms. I have enlarged them, both in number, and weight; so that they are indeed a new work. I thought it therefore agreeable, to my affection, and obligation to your Grace, to prefix your name before them, both in English, and in Latin. For I do conceive, that the Latin volume of them (being in the universal language) may last, as long as books last. My *Instauration*, I dedicated to the King: my *History of Henry the Seventh* (which I have now also translated into Latin) and my portions of *Natural History*, to the Prince: and these I dedicate to your Grace; being of the best fruits, that by the good increase, which God gives to my pen and labours, I could yield. God lead your Grace by the hand.

Your Grace's most obliged and faithful servant,

FRANCIS ST ALBAN

1

Of Truth

What is truth; said jesting Pilate; and would not stay for an answer. Certainly there be, that delight in giddiness; and count it a bondage, to fix a belief; affecting free-will in thinking, as well as in acting. And though the sects of philosophers of that kind be gone, yet there remain certain discoursing wits, which are of the same veins, though there be not so much blood in them, as was in those of the ancients. But it is not only the difficulty, and labour, which men take in finding out of truth; nor again, that when it is found, it imposeth upon men s thoughts; that doth bring lies in favour: but a natural, though corrupt love, of the lie itself. One of the later school of the Grecians, examineth the matter, and is at a stand, to think what should be in it, that men should love lies; where neither they make for pleasure, as with poets; nor for advantage, as with the merchant; but for the lie's sake. But I cannot tell: this same truth, is a naked, and open day light, that doth not show, the masques, and mummeries, and triumphs of the world, half so stately, and daintily, as candlelights. Truth may perhaps come to the price of a pearl, that showeth best by day: but it will not rise, to the price of a diamond, or carbuncle, that showeth best in varied lights. A mixture of a lie doth ever add pleasure. Doth any man doubt, that if there were taken out of men s minds, vain opinions, flattering hopes, false valuations, imaginations as one would, and the like; but it would leave the minds, of a number of men, poor shrunken things; full of melancholy, and indisposition, and unpleasing to themselves? One of the fathers, in great severity, called poesy, *vinum daemonum*; because it filleth the imagination, and yet it is, but with the shadow of a lie. But it is not the lie, that passeth through the mind, but the lie that sinketh in, and settleth in it, that doth the hurt, such as we spake of before. But howsoever these things are thus, in men's depraved judgements, and affections, yet truth, which only doth judge itself, teacheth, that the inquiry of truth, which is the love-making, or wooing of it; the knowledge of truth, which is the presence of it; and the belief of truth, which is the enjoying of it; is the sovereign good of human nature. The first creature of God, in the works of the days, was the light of the sense; the last, was the light of reason; and his Sabbath work, ever since, is the illumination of his spirit. First he breathed light, upon the face, of the matter or chaos; then he breathed light, into the face of man; and still he breatheth and inspireth light, into the face of his chosen. The poet, that beautified the sect, that was otherwise inferior to the rest, saith yet excellently well: 'It is a pleasure to stand upon the shore, and to see ships tossed upon the sea: a pleasure to stand in the window of a castle, and to see a battle, and the adventures thereof, below: but no pleasure is comparable, to the standing, upon the vantage ground of truth:' (a hill not to be commanded, and where the air is always clear and serene;) 'and to see the errors, and wanderings, and mists, and tempests, in the vale below:' so always, that this prospect, be with pity, and not with swelling, or pride. Certainly, it is heaven upon earth, to have a man's mind move in charity, rest in providence, and turn upon the poles of truth.

To pass from theological, and philosophical truth, to the truth of civil business; it will be acknowledged, even by those that practise it not, that clear and round dealing is the honour of man's nature; and that mixture of falsehood, is like allay in coin of gold and silver; which may make the metal work the better, but it embaseth it. For these winding and crooked courses, are the goings of the serpent; which goeth basely upon the belly, and not upon the feet. There is no vice, that doth so cover a man with shame, as to be found false, and perfidious. And therefore Mountaigny saith prettily, when he enquired the reason, why the word of the lie should be such a disgrace, and such an odious charge? saith he, 'If it be well weighed, to lay that a man lieth, is as much to say, as that he is brave towards God, and a coward towards men.' For a lie faces God, and shrinks from man. Surely the wickedness of falsehoods, and breach of faith, cannot possibly be so highly expressed, as in that it shall be the last peal, to call the judgements of God upon the generations of men, it being foretold, that when Christ cometh, He shall not find faith upon the earth.

2

Of Death

Men fear death, as children fear to go in the dark: and as that natural fear in children is increased with tales, so is the other. Certainly, the contemplation of death, as the wages of sin, and passage to another world, is holy and religious; but the fear of it, as a tribute due unto nature, is weak. Yet in religious meditations, there is sometimes mixture of vanity, and of superstition. You shall read, in some of the friars' books of mortifications, that a man should think with himself, what the pain is, if he have but his finger's end pressed, or tortured; and thereby imagine, what the pains of death are, when the whole body is corrupted and dissolved; when many times, death passeth with less pain, then the torture of a limb: for the most vital parts are not the quickest of sense. And by him, that spoke only as a philosopher and natural man, it was well said; *pompa mortis magis terret, quam mors ipsa*. Groans and convulsions, and a discoloured face, and friends weeping, and blacks, and obsequies, and the like, show death terrible. It is worthy the observing, that there is no passion in the mind of man so weak, but it mates, and masters, the fear of death: and therefore death is no such terrible enemy, when a man hath so many attendants about him that can win the combat of him. Revenge triumphs over death; love slights it; honour aspireth to it; grief flieth to it; fear preoccupieth it; nay we read, after Otho the Emperor had slain himself, pity (which is the tenderest of affections) provoked many to die, out of mere compassion to their sovereign, and as the truest sort of followers. Nay, Seneca adds niceness and satiety; *cogita quam diu eadem feceris; mori velle, non tantum fortis, aut miser, sed etiam fastidiosus potest*. A man would die, though he were neither valiant, nor miserable, only upon a weariness to do the same thing, so oft over and over. It is no less worthy to observe, how little alteration, in good spirits, the approaches of death make; for they appear to be the same men, till the last instant. Augustus Caesar died in a compliment; *Livia, coniugii nostri memor, vive et vale*. Tiberius in dissimulation; as Tacitus saith of him; *iam Tiberium vires, et corpus, non dissimulatio, deserebant*. Vespasian in a jest; sitting upon the stool, *ut puto deus fio*. Galba with a sentence; *feri, si ex re sit populi Romani*, holding forth his neck. Septimius Severus in dispatch; *adeste, si quid mihi restat agendum*. And the like. Certainly, the Stoics bestowed too much cost upon death, and by their great preparations, made it appear more fearful. Better saith he, *qui finem vitae extremum inter munera ponat naturae*. It is as natural to die, as to be born; and to a little infant, perhaps, the one is as painful as the other. He that dies in an earnest pursuit, is like one that is wounded in hot blood; who, for the time, scarce feels the hurt; and therefore, a mind fixed, and bent upon somewhat that is good, doth avert the dolours of death: but above all, believe it, the sweetest canticle is, *nunc dimittis*; when a man hath obtained worthy ends, and expectations. Death hath this also; that it openeth the gate to good fame, and extinguisheth envy.

— exstinctus amabitur idem.

3

Of Unity in Religion

Religion being the chief band of human society, it is a happy thing, when itself is well contained within the true band of unity. The quarrels, and divisions about religion, were evils unknown to the heathen. The reason was, because the religion of the heathen consisted rather in rites and ceremonies than in any constant belief. For you may imagine, what kind of faith theirs was, when the chief doctors, and fathers of their church, were the poets. But the true God hath this attribute, that he is a jealous God; and therefore, his worship and religion will endure no mixture, nor partner. We shall therefore speak a few words, concerning the unity of the church; what are the fruits thereof; what the bounds; and what means?

The fruits of unity (next unto the well pleasing of God, which is all in all) are two; the one, towards those that are without the church; the other, towards those that are within. For the former; it is certain, that heresies, and schisms are of all others the greatest scandals; yea more than corruption of manners. For as in the natural body, a wound or solution of continuity is worse than a corrupt humour; so in the spiritual. So that nothing, doth so much keep men out of the church, and drive men out of the church, as breach of unity: and therefore, whensoever it cometh to that pass, that one saith, *ecce in deserto*; another saith, *ecce in penetralibus*; that is, when some men seek Christ in the conventicles of heretics, and others in an outward face of a church, that voice had need continually to sound in men's ears, *nolite exire*, go not out. The doctor of the gentiles (the propriety of whose vocation drew him to have a special care of those without) saith: If an heathen come in and hear you speak with several tongues will he not say that you are mad? And certainly, it is little better when atheists, and profane persons, do hear of so many discordant and contrary opinions in religion; it doth avert them from the church, and maketh them to sit down in the chair of the scorners. It is but a light thing, to be vouched in so serious a matter, but yet it expresseth well the deformity. There is a master of scoffing, that in his catalogue of books, of a feigned library, sets down this title of a book: the morris dance of heretics. For indeed, every sect of them hath a diverse posture, or cringe by themselves, which cannot but move derision in worldlings, and depraved politics, who are apt to contemn holy things.

As for the fruit towards those that are within; it is peace; which containeth infinite blessings: it establisheth faith; it kindleth charity; the outward peace of the church distilleth into peace of conscience; and it turneth the labours of writing, and reading of controversies, into treaties of mortification, and devotion.

Concerning the bounds of unity; the true placing of them importeth exceedingly. There appear to be two extremes. For to certain zealants all speech of pacification is odious. Is it peace, Jehu? What hast thou to do with peace? Turn thee behind me. Peace is not the matter, but following and party. Contrariwise, certain Laodiceans, and lukewarm persons, think they may accommodate points of religion by middle ways, and taking part of both; and witty reconcilements; as if they would make an arbitrement, between God and man. Both these extremes are to be avoided; which will be done, if the league of Christians, penned by our saviour himself, were in the two cross clauses thereof soundly and plainly expounded; he that is not with us, is against us; and again, he that is not against us is with us: that is, if the points fundamental and of substance in religion were truly discerned and distinguished from points not merely of faith, but of opinion, order, or good intention. This is a thing may seem to many a matter trivial, and done already: but if it were done less partially, it would be embraced more generally.

Of this I may give only this advice, according to my small model. Men ought to take heed, of rending God's church, by two kinds of controversies. The one is, when the matter of the point controverted is too small and light, not worth the heat and strife about it, kindled only by contradiction. For, as it is noted by one of the fathers; 'Christ's coat, indeed, had no seam: but the church's vesture was of divers colours;' whereupon he saith, *in veste varietas sit, scissura non sit;* they be two things, unity, and uniformity. The other is, when the matter of the point controverted is great, but it is driven to an over-great subtlety, and obscurity; so that it becometh a thing, rather ingenious, then substantial. A man that is of judgement and under-standing, shall sometimes hear ignorant men differ and know well within himself, that those which so differ, mean one thing, and yet they themselves would never agree. And if it come so to pass, in that distance of judgement which is between man and man, shall we not think, that God above, that knows the heart, doth not discern that frail men, in some of their contradictions, intend the same thing, and accepteth of both? The nature of such controversies is excellently expressed by St Paul, in the warning and precept that he giveth concerning the same, *devita profanas vocum novitates, et oppositiones falsi nominis scientiae*. Men create oppositions, which are not; and put them into new terms, so fixed, as whereas the meaning ought to govern the term, the term in effect governeth the meaning. There be also two false peaces, or unities; the one, when the peace is grounded, but upon an implicit ignorance; for all colours will agree in the dark: the other, when it is pieced up, upon a direct admission of contraries, in fundamental points. For truth and falsehood, in such things, are like the iron and clay in the toes of Nebucadnezzar's image; they may cleave, but they will not incorporate.

Concerning the means of procuring unity; men must beware that in the procuring, or muniting, of religious unity, they do not dissolve and deface the laws of charity, and of human society. There be two swords amongst Christians, the spiritual, and temporal; and both have their due office, and place, in the maintenance of religion. But we may not take up the third sword, which is Mohammed's sword, or like unto it; that is, to propagate religion by wars, or by sanguinary prosecutions, to force consciences; except it be in cases of overt scandal, blasphemy, or intermixture of practice against the state; much less to nourish seditions; to authorise conspiracies and rebel-lions; to put the sword into the people's hands; and the like; tending to the subversion of all government, which is the ordinance of God. For this is but to dash the first table against the second; and so to consider men as Christians, as we forget that they are men. Lucretius the poet, when he beheld the act of Agamemnon, that could endure the sacrificing of his own daughter, exclaimed;

tantum religio potuit suadere malorum.

What would he have said, if he had known of the massacre in France, or the powder treason of England? he would have been seven times more epicure and atheist, than he was. For as the temporal sword is to be drawn with great circumspection, in cases of religion; so it is a thing monstrous, to put it into the hands of the common people. Let that be left unto the Anabaptists, and other furies. It was great blasphemy, when the devil said; I will ascend, and be like the highest; but it is greater blasphemy, to personate God, and bring him in saying; I will descend, and be like the Prince of Darkness; and what, is it better, to make the cause of religion to descend to the cruel and execrable actions of murdering princes, butchery of people, and subversion of states, and governments? Surely, this is to bring down the holy ghost, in stead of the likeness of a dove, in the shape of a vulture, or raven: and to set, out of the bark of a Christian church, a flag of a barque of pirates, and assassins. Therefore it is most necessary, that the church by doctrine and decree; princes by their sword; and all learnings, both Christian and moral, as by their mercury rod; do damn and send to Hell, for ever, those facts and opinions, tending to the support of the same; as hath been already in good part done. Surely in counsels concerning religion, that counsel of the apostle would be prefixed; *ira hominis non implet justitiam dei*. And it was a notable observation, of a wise father, and no less ingenuously confessed; that those, which held and persuaded pressure of consciences were commonly interested therein, themselves, for their own ends.

4

Of Revenge

Revenge is a kind of wild justice; which the more man's nature runs to, the more ought law to weed it out. For as for the first wrong, it doth but offend the law; but the revenge of that wrong, putteth the law out of office. Certainly, in taking revenge, a man is but even with his enemy; but in passing it over, he is superior: for it is a prince's part to pardon. And Solomon, I am sure, saith, It is the glory of a man to pass by an offence. That which is past, is gone, and irrevocable; and wise men have enough to do, with things present, and to come: therefore, they do but trifle with themselves, that labour in past matters. There is no man doth a wrong, for the wrong's sake; but thereby to purchase himself profit, or pleasure, or honour, or the like. Therefore why should I be angry with a man, for loving himself better than me? And if any man should do wrong, merely out of ill nature, why, yet it is but like the thorn, or briar, which prick, and scratch, because they can do no other. The most tolerable sort of revenge, is for those wrongs which there is no law to remedy: but then, let a man take heed the revenge be such as there is no law to punish: else, a man's enemy is still before hand, and it is two for one. Some, when they take revenge, are desirous the party should know whence it cometh: this is the more generous. For the delight seemeth to be, not so much in doing the hurt, as in making the party repent: but base and crafty cowards are like the arrow that flieth in the dark. Cosmus, Duke of Florence, had a desperate saying, against perfidious or neglecting friends, as if those wrongs were unpardonable: You shall read (saith he) that we are commanded to forgive our enemies; but you never read, that we are commanded to forgive our friends. But yet the spirit of Job, was in a better tune; Shall we (saith he) take good at God's hands, and not be content to take evil also? And so of friends in a proportion. This is certain; that a man that studieth revenge, keeps his own wounds green, which otherwise would heal, and do well. Public revenges, are, for the most part, fortunate; as that for the death of Caesar; for the death of Pertinax; for the death of Henry the Third of France; and many more. But in private revenges it is not so. Nay rather, vindictive persons live the life of witches; who as they are mischievous, so end they unfortunate.

5

Of Adversity

It was an high speech of Seneca (after the manner of the Stoics) that the good things which belong to prosperity are to be wished; but the good things that belong to adversity are to be admired. *Bona rerum secundarum optabilia; adversarum mirabilia.* Certainly if miracles be the command over nature, they appear most in adversity. It is yet a higher speech of his than the other (much too high for a heathen): It is true greatness to have in one the fragility of a man and the security of a God. *Vere magnum habere fragilitatem hominis securitatem dei.* This would have done better in poesy; where transcendencies are more allowed. And the poets indeed, have been busy with it; for it is, in effect, the thing which is figured in that strange fiction of the ancient poets, which seemeth not to be without mystery; nay, and to have some approach to the state of a Christian: that Hercules when he went to unbind Prometheus (by whom human nature is represented) sailed the length of the great ocean in an earthen pot or pitcher: lively describing Christian resolution; that saileth, in the frail barque of the flesh, through the waves of the world. But to speak in a mean. The virtue of prosperity is temperance; the virtue of adversity is fortitude: which in morals is the more heroical virtue. Prosperity is the blessing of the Old Testament; adversity is the blessing of the New; which carrieth the greater benediction, and the clearer revelation of God's favour. Yet, even in the Old Testament, if you listen to David's harp, you shall hear as many hearselike airs, as carols: and the pencil of the Holy Ghost hath laboured more, in describing the afflictions of Job, than the felicities of Solomon. Prosperity is not without many fears and distastes; and adversity is not without comforts and hopes. We see in needlework, and embroideries, it is more pleasing to have a lively work upon a sad and solemn ground, than to have a dark and melancholy work, upon a lightsome ground: judge therefore, of the pleasure of the heart, by the pleasure of the eye. Certainly, virtue is like precious odours, most fragrant when they are incensed, or crushed: for prosperity doth best discover vice; but adversity doth best discover virtue.

6

Of Simulation & Dissimulation

Dissimulation is but a faint kind of policy, or wisdom; for it asketh a strong wit, and a strong heart, to know when to tell truth, and to do it. Therefore it is the weaker sort of politics, that are the great dissemblers.

Tacitus saith; Livia sorted well, with the arts of her husband, and dissimulation of her son: attributing arts or policy to Augustus, and dissimulation to Tiberius. And again, when Lucianus encourageth Vespasian, to take arms against Vitellius, he saith; We rise not, against the piercing judgment of Augustus, nor the extreme caution or closeness of Tiberius. These properties of arts or policy, and dissimulation or closeness, are indeed habits and faculties, several, and to be distinguished. For if a man have that penetration of judgment, as he can discern, what things are to be laid open, and what to be secreted, and what to be showed at half lights, and to whom, and when (which indeed are arts of state, and arts of life, as Tacitus well calleth them), to him, a habit of dissimulation is a hindrance, and a poorness. But if a man cannot obtain to that judgment, then it is left to him, generally, to be close, and a dissembler. For where a man cannot choose, or vary in particulars, there it is good to take the safest and wariest way in general; like the going softly by one that cannot well see. Certainly the ablest men that ever were, have had all an openness, and frankness of dealing; and a name of certainty, and veracity; but then they were like horses, well managed; for they could tell passing well when to stop, or turn: and at such times, when they thought the case indeed required dissimulation, if then they used it, it came to pass, that the former opinion, spread abroad of their good faith, and clearness of dealing, made them almost invisible.

There be three degrees, of this hiding and veiling of a man's self.

The first closeness, reservation, and secrecy; when a man leaveth himself without observation, or without hold to be taken, what he is. The second dissimulation, in the negative; when a man lets fall signs, and arguments, that he is not, that he is. And the third simulation, in the affirmative; when a man industriously, and expressly, feigns and pretends to be that he is not.

For the first of these, secrecy: it is indeed, the virtue of a confessor; and assuredly, the secret man heareth many confessions; for who will open himself to a blab or a babbler? But if a man be thought secret, it inviteth discovery; as the more close air, sucketh in the more open: and as in confession, the revealing is not for worldly use, but for the ease of a man's heart, so secret men come to the knowledge of many things, in that kind; while men rather discharge their minds, than impart their minds. In few words, mysteries are due to secrecy. Besides (to say truth) nakedness is uncomely, as well in mind, as body; and it addeth no small reverence, to men's manners, and actions, if they be not altogether open. As for talkers and futile persons, they are commonly vain, and credulous withal. For he that talketh what he knoweth, will also talk what he knoweth not. Therefore set it down; that an habit of secrecy is both politic and moral. And in this part, it is good, that a man's face give his tongue leave to speak. For the discovery of a man's self by the tracts of his countenance, is a great weakness, and betraying; by how much, it is many times more marked and believed, than a man's words.

For the second, which is dissimulation. It followeth many times upon secrecy, by a necessity: so that, he that will be secret, must be a dissembler, in some degree. For men are too cunning, to suffer a man to keep an indifferent carriage between both, and to be secret, without swaying the balance, on either side. They will so beset a man with questions, and draw him on, and pick it out of him, that without an absurd silence, he must show an inclination, one way; or if he do not, they will gather as much by his silence, as by his speech. As for equivocations, or oraculous speeches, they cannot hold out long. So that no man can be secret, except he give himself a little scope of dissimulation; which is, as it were, but the skirts or train of secrecy.

But for the third degree, which is simulation, and false profession; that I hold more culpable, and less politic; except it be in great and rare matters. And therefore a general custom of simulation (which is this last degree) is a vice, rising either of a natural falseness, or fearfulness; or of a mind, that hath some main faults; which because a man must needs disguise, it maketh him practise simulation in other things, lest his hand should be out of use.

The great advantages of simulation and dissimulation are three. First to lay asleep opposition, and to surprise. For where a man's intentions are published, it is an alarum, to call up all that are against them. The second is, to reserve to a man's self a fair retreat: for if a man engage himself, by a manifest declaration, he must go through, or take a fall. The third is, the better to discover the mind of another. For to him that opens himself, men will hardly show themselves adverse; but will (fair) let him go on, and turn their freedom of speech, to freedom of thought. And therefore, it is a good shrewd proverb of the Spaniard; tell a lie, and find a troth. As if there were no way of discovery, but by simulation. There be also three disadvantages, to set it even. The first, that simulation and dissimulation commonly carry with them a show of fearfulness, which in any business doth spoil the feathers, of round flying up to the mark. The second, that it puzzleth and perplexeth the conceits of many that perhaps would otherwise co-operate with him; and makes a man walk, almost alone, to his own ends. The third, and greatest is, that it depriveth a man of one of the most principal instruments for action; which is trust and belief. The best composition and temperature is to have openness in fame and opinion; secrecy in habit; dissimulation in seasonable use; and a power to feign, if there be no remedy.

7

Of Parents & Children

The joys of parents are secret; and so are their griefs, and fears: they cannot utter the one; nor they will not utter the other. Children sweeten labours; but they make misfortunes more bitter: they increase the cares of life; but they mitigate the remembrance of death. The perpetuity by generation is common to beasts; but memory, merit, and noble works, are proper to men: and surely a man shall see the noblest works and foundations have proceeded from childless men; which have sought to express the images of their minds where those of their bodies have failed: so the care of posterity is most in them that have no posterity. They that are the first raisers of their houses, are most indulgent towards their children; beholding them, as the continuance, not only of their kind, but of their work; and so both children and creatures.

The difference in affection of parents towards their several children is many times unequal; and sometimes unworthy; especially in the mother; as Solomon saith; A wise son rejoiceth the father; but an ungracious son shames the mother. A man shall see, where there is a house full of children, one or two of the eldest respected, and the youngest made wantons; but in the midst, some that are, as it were forgotten, who many times, nevertheless, prove the best. The illiberality of parents, in allowance towards their children, is an harmful error; makes them base; acquaints them with shifts; makes them sort with mean company; and makes them surfeit more, when they come to plenty: and therefore, the proof is best, when men keep their authority towards their children, but not their purse. Men have a foolish manner (both parents, and schoolmasters, and servants) in creating and breeding an emulation between brothers, during child-hood, which many times sorteth to discord, when they are men; and disturbeth families. The Italians make little difference between children, and nephews, or near kinsfolk; but so they be of the lump, they care not, though they passe not through their own body. And, to say truth, in nature it is much a like matter; in so much, that we see a nephew sometimes resembleth an uncle, or a kinsman, more then his own parent; as the blood happens. Let parents choose betimes the vocations and courses they mean their children should take; for then they are most flexible; and let them not too much apply themselves to the disposition of their children, as thinking they will take best to that, which they have most mind to. It is true, that if the affection or aptness of the children be extraordinary, then it is good not to cross it; but generally, the precept is good; *optimum elige, suave et facile illud faciet consuetudo.* Younger brothers are commonly fortunate, but seldom or never where the elder are disinherited.

8

Of Marriage & Single Life

He that hath wife and children, hath given hostages to fortune; for they are impediment to great enterprises, either of virtue, or mischief. Certainly, the best works, and of greatest merit for the public, have proceeded from the unmarried or childless men; which both in affection, and means, have married and endowed the public. Yet it were great reason, that those that have children, should have greatest care of future times; unto which, they know, they must transmit their dearest pledges. Some there are, who though they lead a single life, yet their thoughts do end with themselves, and account future times impertinences. Nay, there are some other, that account wife and children but as bills of charges. Nay more, there are some foolish rich covetous men, that take a pride in having no children, because they may be thought so much the richer. For perhaps, they have heard some talk; Such an one is a great rich man; and another except to it; Yea, but he hath a great charge of children: as if it were an abatement to his riches. But the most ordinary cause of a single life is liberty; especially in certain self-pleasing and humorous minds, which are so sensible of every restraint, as they will go near to think their girdles and garters to be bonds and shackles. Unmarried men are best friends; best masters; best servants; but not always best subjects; for they are light to run away; and almost all fugitives are of that condition. A single life doth well with church men: for charity will hardly water the ground, where it must first fill a pool. It is indifferent for judges and magistrates: for if they be facile, and corrupt, you shall have a servant five times worse than a wife. For soldiers, I find the generals commonly in their hortatives, put men in mind of their wives and children: and I think the despising of marriage amongst the Turks, maketh the vulgar soldier more base. Certainly, wife and children are a kind of discipline of humanity: and single men though they be many times more charitable, because their means are less exhaust; yet, on the other side, they are more cruel, and hard hearted (good to make severe inquisitors), because their tenderness is not so oft called upon. Grave natures, led by custom, and therefore constant, are commonly loving husbands; as was said of Ulysses; *vetulam suam praetulit immortalitati*. Chaste women are often proud and forward, as presuming upon the merit of their chastity. It is one of the best bonds, both of chastity and obedience, in the wife, if she think her husband wise; which she will never do, if she find him jealous. Wives are young men's mistresses; companions for middle age; and old men's nurses. So as a man may have a quarrel to marry, when he will. But yet, he was reputed one of the wise men, that made answer to the question, when a man should marry? A young man not yet, an elder man not at all. It is often seen, that bad husbands have very good wives; whether it be, that it raiseth the price of their husband's kindness, when it comes; or that the wives take a pride in their patience. But this never fails, if the bad husbands were of their own choosing, against their friends' consent; for then, they will be sure to make good their own folly.

9

Of Envy

There be none of the affections, which have been noted to fascinate or bewitch, but love, and envy. They both have vehement wishes; they frame themselves readily into imaginations, and suggestions; and they come easily into the eye; especially upon the presence of the objects; which are the points that conduce to fascination, if any such thing there be. We see likewise, the scripture calleth envy an evil eye: and the astrologers call the evil influences of the stars, evil aspects; so that still, there seemeth to be acknowledged, in the act of envy, an ejaculation or irradiation of the eye. Nay, some have been so curious as to note, that the times, when the stroke, or percussion of an envious eye doth most hurt, are when the party envied is beheld in glory, or triumph; for that sets an edge upon envy; and besides, at such times, the spirit of the person envied do come forth most into the outward parts, and so meet the blow.

But leaving these curiosities (though not unworthy, to be thought on, in fit place), we will handle, what persons are apt to envy others; what persons are most subject to be envied themselves; and, what is the difference between public and private envy.

A man that hath no virtue in himself, ever envieth virtue in others. For men's minds will either feed upon their own good, or upon others' evil; and who wanteth the one, will prey upon the other; and who so is out of hope to attain to another's virtue, will seek to come at even hand, by depressing another's fortune.

A man that is busy, and inquisitive, is commonly envious: for to know much of other men's matters, cannot be, because all that ado may concern his own estate: therefore it must needs be, that he taketh a kind of play-pleasure, in looking upon the fortunes of others; neither can he, that mindeth but his own business, find much matter for envy. For envy is a gadding passion, and walketh the streets, and doth not keep home; *non est curiosus, quin idem sit malevolus*.

Men of noble birth are noted to be envious towards new men, when they rise. For the distance is altered; and it is like a deceit of the eye, that when others come on, they think themselves go back.

Deformed persons, and eunuchs, and old men, and bastards, are envious: for he that cannot possibly mend his own case, will do what he can to impair another's; except these defects light upon a very brave and heroical nature; which thinketh to make his natural wants, part of his honour: in that it should be said, that an eunuch, or a lame man, did such great matters; affecting the honour of a miracle; as it was in Narses the eunuch, and Agesilaus, and Tamberlanes, that were lame men.

The same is the case of men that rise after calamities, and misfortunes; for they are, as men fallen out with the times; and think other men's harms a redemption of their own sufferings.

They that desire to excel in too many matters, out of levity and vain glory, are ever envious; for they cannot want work; it being impossible, but many, in some one of those things, should surpass them. Which was the character of Hadrian the Emperor, that mortally envied poets, and painters, and artificers, in works wherein he had a vein to excel.

Lastly, near kinsfolk, and fellows in office, and those that have been bred together, are more apt to envy their equals, when they are raised. For it doth upbraid unto them their own fortunes; and pointeth at them, and cometh oftener into their remembrance, and incurreth likewise more into the note of others: and envy ever redoubleth from speech and fame. Cain's envy was the more vile and malignant, towards his brother Abel, because, when his sacrifice was better accepted, there was nobody to look on. Thus much for those that are apt to envy.

Concerning those that are more or less subject to envy: first, persons of eminent virtue, when they are advanced, are less envied. For their fortune seemeth but due unto them; and no man envieth the payment of a debt, but rewards and liberality rather. Again, envy is ever joined with the comparing of a man's self; and where there is no comparison, no envy; and therefore kings are not envied but by kings. Nevertheless, it is to be noted, that unworthy persons are most envied at their first coming in, and afterwards overcome it better;

whereas contrariwise, persons of worth and merit are most envied when their fortune continueth long. For by that time, though their virtue be the same, yet it hath not the same lustre; for fresh men grow up, that darken it.

Persons of noble blood are less envied in their rising: for it seemeth but right, done to their birth. Besides, there seemeth not much added to their fortune; and envy is as the sunbeams, that beat hotter upon a bank or steep rising ground than upon a flat. And for the same reason, those that are advanced by degrees are less envied than those that are advanced suddenly, and *per saltum*.

Those that have joined with their honour, great travels, cares, or perils, are less subject to envy. For men think, that they earn their honours hardly, and pity them sometimes; and pity ever healeth envy: wherefore, you shall observe that the more deep and sober sort of politic persons, in their greatness, are ever bemoaning themselves, what a life they lead; chanting a *quanta patimur*. Not that they feel it so, but only to abate the edge of envy. But this is to be understood, of business that is laid upon men, and not such as they call unto themselves. For nothing increaseth envy more, than an unnecessary and ambitious engrossing of business. And nothing doth extinguish envy more, than for a great person to preserve all other inferior officers, in their full rights, and pre-eminence of their places. For by that means, there be so many screens between him and envy.

Above all, those are most subject to envy, which carry the greatness of their fortunes in an insolent and proud manner: being never well, but while they are showing how great they are, either by outward pomp, or by triumphing over all opposition, or competition; whereas wise men will rather do sacrifice to envy; in suffering themselves, sometimes of purpose to be crossed, and overborne in things, that do not much concern them. Notwithstanding, so much is true; that the carriage of greatness, in a plain and open manner (so it be without arrogance, and vain glory) doth draw less envy, than if it be in a more crafty and cunning fashion. For in that course, a man doth but disavow fortune; and seemeth to be conscious of his own want in worth; and doth but teach others to envy him.

Lastly, to conclude this part; as we said in the beginning, that the act of envy, had somewhat in it, of witchcraft; so there is no other cure of envy, but the cure of witchcraft: and that is, to remove the lot (as they call it) and to lay it upon another. For which purpose, the wiser sort of great persons bring in ever upon the stage somebody, upon whom to derive the envy, that would come upon themselves; sometimes upon ministers, and servants; sometimes upon colleagues and associates; and the like; and for that turn, there are never wanting, some persons of violent and undertaking natures, who so they may have power, and business, will take it at any cost.

Now to speak of public envy. There is yet some good in public envy; whereas in private, there is none. For public envy is as an ostracism, that eclipseth men, when they grow too great. And therefore it is a bridle also to great ones, to keep them within bounds.

This envy, being in the Latin word *invidia*, goeth in the modern languages, by the name of discontentment: of which we shall speak in handling sedition. It is a disease, in a state, like to infection. For as infection spreadeth upon that which is sound, and tainteth it; so when envy is gotten once into a state, it traduceth even the best actions thereof, and turneth them into an ill odour. And therefore, there is little won by intermingling of plausible actions. For that doth argue but a weakness, and fear of envy, which hurteth so much the more, as it is likewise usual in infections; which if you fear them, you call them upon you.

This public envy seemeth to beat chiefly upon principal officers, or ministers, rather than upon kings, and estates themselves. But this is a sure rule, that if the envy upon the minister be great, when the cause of it in him is small; or if the envy be general, in a manner, upon all the ministers of an estate; then the envy (though hidden) is truly upon the estate itself. And so much of public envy or discontentment, and the difference thereof from private envy, which was handled in the first place.

We will add this, in general, touching the affection of envy; that of all other affections, it is the most importune, and continual. For of other affections, there is occasion given, but now and then: and therefore, it was well said, *invidia festos dies non agit*. For it is ever working upon some or other. And it is also noted, that love and envy do make a man pine. Which other affections do not; because they are not so continual. It is also the vilest affection, and the most depraved; for which cause, it is the proper attribute of the devil, who is called: the envious man, that soweth tares amongst the wheat by night. As it always cometh to pass, that envy worketh subtly, and in the dark; and to the prejudice of good things, such as is the wheat.

10

Of Love

The stage is more beholding to love, than the life of man. For as to the stage, love is ever matter of comedies, and now and then of tragedies: but in life, it doth much mischief: sometimes like a siren; sometimes like a fury. You may observe, that amongst all the great and worthy persons (whereof the memory remaineth, either ancient or recent) there is not one, that hath been transported to the mad degree of love: which shows, that great spirits, and great business, do keep out this weak passion. You must except, nevertheless, Marcus Antonius the half partner of the empire of Rome; and Appius Claudius the *decemvir*, and lawgiver: whereof the former was indeed a voluptuous man, and inordinate; but the latter was an austere and wise man: and therefore it seems (though rarely) that love can find entrance, not only into an open heart; but also into a heart well fortified, if watch be not well kept. It is a poor saying of Epicurus, *satis magnum alter alteri theatrum sumus*: as if man, made for the contemplation of heaven and all noble objects, should do nothing, but kneel before a little idol, and make himself subject, though not of the mouth (as beasts are) yet of the eye; which was given him for higher purposes. It is a strange thing, to note the excess of this passion; and how it braves the nature and value of things; by this, that the speaking in a perpetual hyperbole is comely in nothing but in love. Neither is it merely in the phrase; for whereas it hath been well said, that the arch-flatterer, with whom all the petty flatterers have intelligence, is a man's self; certainly, the lover is more. For there was never proud man thought so absurdly well of himself, as the lover doth of the person loved: and therefore, it was well said; that it is impossible to love, and to be wise. Neither doth this weakness appear to others only, and not to the party loved; but to the loved, most of all: except the love be reciproque. For it is a true rule, that love is ever rewarded, either with the reciproque, or with an inward and secret contempt. By how much the more, men ought to beware of this passion, which loseth not only other things, but itself. As for the other losses, the poet's relation doth well figure them; that he that preferred Helena, quitted the gifts of Juno, and Pallas. For whosoever esteemeth too much of amorous affection, quitteth both riches, and wisdom. This passion hath his floods in the very times of weakness; which are, great prosperity; and great adversity; though this latter hath been less observed. Both which times kindle love, and make it more fervent, and therefore show it to be the child of folly. They do best, who, if they cannot but admit love, yet make it keep quarter: and sever it wholly from their serious affairs, and actions of life: for if it check once with business, it troubleth men s fortunes, and maketh men, that they can no ways be true to their own ends. I know not how, but martial men are given to love: I think it is, but as they are given to wine; for perils commonly ask to be paid in pleasures. There is in man's nature, a secret inclination, and motion, towards love of others; which, if it be not spent upon some one, or a few, doth naturally spread itself towards many; and maketh men become humane, and charitable; as it is seen sometime in friars. Nuptial love maketh mankind; friendly love perfecteth it; but wanton love corrupteth and embaseth it.

11

Of Great Place

Men in great place, are thrice servants: servants of the sovereign or state; servants of fame; and servants of business. So as they have no freedom; neither in their persons; nor in their actions; nor in their times. It is a strange desire, to seek power, and to lose liberty; or to seek power over others, and to lose power over a man's self. The rising unto place is laborious; and by pains men come to greater pains; and it is sometimes base; and by indignities, men come to dignities. The standing is slippery, and the regress is either a downfall, or at least an eclipse, which is a melancholy thing. *Cum non sis, qui fueris, non esse, cur velis vivere*. Nay, retire men cannot, when they would; neither will they, when it were reason: but are impatient of privateness, even in age, and sickness, which require the shadow: like old townsmen, that will be still sitting at their street door; though thereby they offer age to scorn. Certainly great persons had need to borrow other men's opinions, to think themselves happy; for if they judge by their own feeling, they cannot find it: but if they think with themselves, what other men think of them, and that other men would fain be as they are, then they are happy, as it were by report; when perhaps they find the contrary within. For they are the first that find their own griefs; though they be the last that find their own faults. Certainly, men in great fortunes are strangers to themselves, and while they are in the pulse of business, they have no time to tend their health, either of body, or mind. *Illi mors gravis incubat, qui notus nimis omnibus, ignotus moritur sibi*. In place, there is licence to do good, and evil; whereof the latter is a curse; for in evil, the best condition is, not to will; the second, not to can. But power to do good, is the true and lawful end of aspiring. For good thoughts (though God accept them), yet towards men, are little better then good dreams; except they be put in act; and that cannot be without power, and place; as the vantage, and commanding ground. Merit, and good works, is the end of man's motion; and conscience of the same is the accomplishment of man's rest. For if a man can be partaker of God's theatre, he shall likewise be partaker of God's rest. *Et conversus Deus, ut aspiceret opera quae fecerunt manus suae, vidit quod omnia essent bona nimis;* and then the Sabbath. In the discharge of thy place, set before thee the best examples; for imitation is a globe of precepts. And after a time, set before thee thine own example; and examine thy self strictly, whether thou didst not best at first. Neglect not also the examples of those that have carried themselves ill in the same place: not to set off thy self, by taxing their memory; but to direct thy self, what to avoid. Reform therefore, without bravery, or scandal, of former times, and persons; but yet set it down to thyself, as well to create good precedents, as to follow them. Reduce things to the first institution, and observe wherein, and how, they have degenerate; but yet ask counsel of both times; of the ancient time, what is best; and of the latter time, what is fittest. Seek to make thy course regular; that men may know beforehand what they may expect: but be not too positive, and peremptory; and express thyself well, when thou digressest from thy rule. Preserve the right of thy place; but stir not questions of jurisdiction: and rather assume thy right in silence and *de facto*, than voice it with claims and challenges. Preserve likewise, the rights of inferior places; and think it more honour to direct in chief, than to be busy in all. Embrace and invite helps, and advices, touching the execution of thy place; and do not drive away such as bring thee information, as meddlers; but accept of them in good part. The vices of authority are chiefly four: delays; corruption; roughness; and facility. For delays; give easy access; keep times appointed; go through with that which is in hand; and interlace not business, but of necessity. For corruption; do not only bind thine own hands, or thy servants' hands, from taking; but bind the hands of suitors also from offering. For integrity used doth the one; but integrity professed, and with a manifest detestation of bribery, doth the other. And avoid not only the fault, but the suspicion. Whosoever is found variable, and changeth manifestly, without manifest cause, giveth suspicion of corruption. Therefore, always, when thou changest thine opinion, or course, profess it plainly, and declare it, together with the reasons that move thee to change; and do not think to steal it. A servant, or a favourite, if he be inward, and no other apparent cause of esteem, is commonly thought but a by-way, to close corruption. For roughness; it is a needless cause of discontent: severity breedeth fear, but roughness breedeth hate. Even reproofs from authority ought to be grave, and not taunting. As for facility; it is worse then bribery. For bribes come but now and then; but if importunity or idle respects lead a man, he shall never be without. As Solomon saith; to respect persons is not good; for such a man will transgress for a peace of bread. It is most true, that was anciently spoken; A place sheweth the man: and it showeth some to the better, and some to the worse: *omnium consensu, capax imperii, nisi imperasset*; saith Tacitus of Galba: but of Vespasian he saith; *solus imperantium Vespasianus mutatus in melius*. Though the one was meant of sufficiency, the other of manners, and affection. It is an assured sign of a worthy and generous spirit, whom honour amends. For honour is, or should be, the place of virtue: and as in nature things move violently to their place, and calmly in their place: so virtue in ambition is violent, in authority settled and calm. All rising to great place is by a winding stair: and if there be factions, it is good to side a man's self, whilst he is in the rising; and to balance himself, when he is placed. Use the memory of thy predecessor fairly, and tenderly; for if thou dost not, it is a debt will sure be paid, when thou art gone. If thou have colleagues, respect them, and rather call them, when they look not for it, than exclude them, when they have reason to look to be called. Be not too sensible, or too remembering, of thy place in conversation and private answers to suitors; but let it rather be said; When he sits in place, he is another man.

12

Of Boldness

It is a trivial grammar school text, but yet worthy a wise man's consideration. Question was asked of Demosthenes; what was the chief part of an orator? He answered, Action; what next? Action; what next again? Action. He said it, that knew it best; and had by nature, himself, no advantage in that he commended. A strange thing, that that part of an orator, which is but superficial, and rather the virtue of a player, should be placed so high, above those other noble parts, of invention, elocution, and the rest: nay almost alone, as if it were all in all. But the reason is plain. There is in human nature, generally, more of the fool than of the wise, and therefore those faculties, by which the foolish part of men's minds is taken, are most potent. Wonderful like is the case of boldness in civil business; what first? Boldness; what second, and third? Boldness. And yet boldness is a child of ignorance and baseness, far inferior to other parts. But nevertheless, it doth fascinate, and bind hand and foot, those that are either shallow in judgment, or weak in courage, which are the greatest part; yea, and prevaileth with wise men, at weak times. Therefore, we see it hath done wonders, in popular states; but with senates and princes less; and more ever upon the first entrance of bold persons into action, than soon after; for boldness is an ill keeper of promise. Surely, as there are mountebanks for the natural body, so are there mountebanks for the political body: men that undertake great cures; and perhaps have been lucky, in two or three experiments, but want the grounds of science; and therefore cannot hold out. Nay you shall see a bold fellow, many times, do Mohammed's miracle. Mohammed made the people believe, that he would call an hill to him; and from the top of it, offer up his prayers, for the observers of his law. The people assembled; Mohammed called the hill to come to him, again, and again; and when the hill stood still, he was never a whit abashed, but said; if the hill will not come to Mohammed, Mohammed must go to the hill. So these men, when they have promised great matters, and failed most shamefully, (yet if they have the perfection of boldness) they will but slight it over, and make a turn, and no more ado. Certainly, to men of great judgment, bold persons are a sport to behold; nay, and to the vulgar also, boldness hath somewhat of the ridiculous. For if absurdity be the subject of laughter, doubt you not, but great boldness is seldom without some absurdity. Especially, it is a sport to see, when a bold fellow is out of countenance; for that puts his face into a most shrunken and wooden posture; as needs it must; for in bashfulness, the spirits do a little go and come; but with bold men, upon like occasion, they stand at a stay; like a stale at chess, where it is no mate, but yet the game cannot stir. But this last, were fitter for a satire, than for a serious observation. This is well to be weighed; that boldness is ever blind: for it seeth not dangers and inconveniences. Therefore, it is ill in counsel, good in execution: so that the right use of bold persons is, that they never command in chief, but be seconds, and under the direction of others. For in counsel, it is good to see dangers; and in execution, not to see them, except they be very great.

13

Of Goodness, & Goodness of Nature

I take goodness in this sense, the affecting of the weal of men, which is that the Grecians call philanthropia; and the word humanity (as it is used) is a little too light, to express it. Goodness I call the habit, and goodness of nature the inclination. This of all virtues, and dignities of the mind, is the greatest; being the character of the deity: and without it, man is a busy, mischievous, wretched thing; no better than a kind of vermin. Goodness answers to the theological virtue charity, and admits no excess, but error. The desire of power in excess, caused the angels to fall; the desire of knowledge in excess, caused man to fall; but in charity, there is no excess; neither can angel, or man, come in danger by it. The inclination to goodness is imprinted deeply in the nature of man: in so much, that if it issue not towards men, it will take unto other living creatures: as it is seen in the Turks, a cruel people, who nevertheless are kind to beasts, and give alms to dogs, and birds: in so much, as Busbechius reporteth; a Christian boy in Constantinople had like to have been stoned, for gagging, in a waggishness, a long billed fowl. Errors, indeed, in this virtue of goodness, or charity, may be committed. The Italians have an ungracious proverb; *tanto buon che val niente*: so good, that he is good for nothing. And one of the doctors of Italy, Nicholas Machiavelli, had the confidence to put in writing, almost in plain terms: That the Christian faith had given up good men, in prey, to those that are tyrannical, and unjust. Which he spoke, because indeed there was never law, or sect, or opinion, did so much magnify goodness, as the Christian religion doth. Therefore to avoid the scandal, and the danger both, it is good to take knowledge of the errors of an habit so excellent. Seek the good of other men, but be not in bondage to their faces, or fancies; for that is but facility, or softness; which taketh an honest mind prisoner. Neither give thou Aesop's cock a gem, who would be better pleased, and happier, if he had had a barley corn. The example of God teacheth the lesson truly: he sendeth his rain, and maketh his sun to shine, upon the just, and unjust; but he doth not rain wealth, nor shine honour, and virtues, upon men equally. Common benefits are to be communicate with all; but peculiar benefits, with choice. And beware, how in making the portraiture, thou breakest the pattern: for divinity maketh the love of ourselves the pattern; the love of our neighbours but the portraiture. Sell all thou hast, and give it to the poor, and follow me: but sell not all thou hast, except thou come, and follow me; that is, except thou have a vocation, wherein thou may do as much good with little means as with great: for otherwise, in feeding the streams, thou driest the fountain. Neither is there only a habit of goodness, directed by right reason; but there is, in some men, even in nature, a disposition towards it: as on the other side, there is a natural malignity. For there be, that in their nature do not affect the good of others. The lighter sort of malignity, turneth but to a crossness, or forwardness, or aptness to oppose, or difficultness, or the like; but the deeper sort, to envy, and mere mischief. Such men, in other men's calamities, are, as it were, in season, and are ever on the loading part; not so good as the dogs that licked Lazarus's sores; but like flies, that are still buzzing upon anything that is raw; *misanthropi*, that make it their practice, to bring men to the bough; and yet have never a tree for the purpose, in their gardens, as Timon had. Such dispositions are the very errors of human nature: and yet they are the fittest timber, to make great politics of: like to knee timber, that is good for ships that are ordained to be tossed; but not for building houses, that shall stand firm. The parts and signs of goodness are many. If a man be gracious, and courteous to strangers, it shows he is a citizen of the world; and that his heart is no island, cut off from other lands; but a continent, that joins to them. If he be compassionate towards the afflictions of others, it shows that his heart is like the noble tree, that is wounded itself, when it gives the balm. If he easily pardons and remits offences, it shows that his mind is planted above injuries; so that he cannot be shot. If he be thankful for small benefits, it shows that he weighs men's minds, and not their trash. But above all, if he have St Paul's perfection, that he would wish to be an anathema from Christ, for the salvation of his brethren, it shows much of a divine nature, and a kind of conformity with Christ himself.

14

Of Nobility

We will speak of nobility, first as a portion of an estate; then as a condition of particular persons. A monarchy, where there is no nobility at all, is ever a pure and absolute tyranny; as that of the Turks. For nobility attempers sovereignty, and draws the eyes of the people somewhat aside from the line royal. But for democracies, they need it not; and they are commonly more quiet, and less subject to sedition, then where there are stirps of nobles. For men's eyes are upon the business, and not upon the persons: or if upon the persons, it is for the business' sake, as fittest, and not for flags and pedigree. We see the Switzers last well, notwithstanding their diversity of religion, and of cantons. For utility is their bond, and not respects. The united provinces of the Low Countries, in their government, excel: for where there is an equality, the consultations are more indifferent, and the payments and tributes more cheerful. A great and potent nobility addeth majesty to a monarch, but diminisheth power; and putteth life and spirit into the people, but presseth their fortune. It is well, when nobles are not too great for sovereignty, nor for justice; and yet maintained in that height, as the insolence of inferiors may be broken upon them, before it come on too fast upon the majesty of kings. A numerous nobility causeth poverty and inconvenience in a state: for it is a surcharge of expense; and besides, it being of necessity, that many of the nobility fall in time to be weak in fortune, it maketh a kind of disproportion, between honour and means.

As for nobility in particular persons; it is a reverend thing, to see an ancient castle or building not in decay; or to see a fair timber tree, sound and perfect: how much more, to behold an ancient noble family, which hath stood against the waves and weathers of time. For new nobility is but the act of power; but ancient nobility is the act of time. Those that are first raised to nobility are commonly more virtuous, but less innocent, than their descendants: for there is rarely any rising, but by a co-mixture, of good and evil arts. But it is reason the memory of their virtues remain to their posterity; and their faults die with themselves. Nobility of birth commonly abateth industry: and he that is not industrious envieth him that is. Besides, noble persons cannot go much higher; and he that standeth at a stay, when others rise, can hardly avoid motions of envy. On the other side, nobility extinguisheth the passive envy, from others towards them; because they are in possession of honour. Certainly kings, that have able men of their nobility, shall find ease in employing them; and a better slide into their business: for people naturally bend to them, as born in some sort to command.

15

Of Seditions & Troubles

Shepherds of people had need know the calendars of tempests in state; which are commonly greatest, when things grow to equality; as natural tempests are greatest about the equinoxes. And as there are certain hollow blasts of wind, and secret swellings of seas, before a tempest, so are there in states:

> *ille etiam caecos instare tumultus*
> *saepe monet, fraudesque et operta tumescere bella.*

Libels, and licentious discourses against the state, when they are frequent and open; and in like sort, false news, often running up and down, to the disadvantage of the state, and hastily embraced; are amongst the signs of troubles. Virgil giving the pedigree of fame, saith, she was sister to the giants.

> *Illam terra parens ira irritata deorum,*
> *extremam (ut perhibent) Coeo Enceladoque sororem*
> *progenuit.*

As if fame were the relics of seditions past; but they are no less, indeed, the preludes of seditions to come. Howsoever, he noteth it right, that seditious tumults and seditious fame differ no more, but as brother and sister, masculine and feminine; especially, if it come to that, that the best actions of a state, and the most plausible, and which ought to give greatest contentment, are taken in ill sense, and traduced: for that shows the envy great, as Tacitus saith; *conflata magna invidia, seu bene, seu male, gesta premunt*. Neither doth it follow, that because these fames are a sign of troubles, that the suppressing of them with too much severity, should be a remedy of troubles. For the despising of them, many times, checks them best; and the going about to stop them, doth but make a wonder long-lived. Also that kind of obedience, which Tacitus speaketh of, is to be held suspected; *erant in officio, sed tamen qui mallent mandata imperantium interpretari, quam exsequi*; disputing, excusing, calling upon mandates and directions, is a kind of shaking off the yoke, and assay of disobedience: especially, if in those disputings they which are for the direction, speak fearfully, and tenderly; and those that are against it, audaciously.

Also, as Machiavelli noteth well; when princes, that ought to be common parents, make themselves as a party, and lean to a side, it is as a boat that is overthrown by uneven weight on the one side; as was well seen, in the time of Henry the Third of France: for first, himself entered league for the extirpation of the Protestants; and presently after, the same league was turned upon himself. For when the authority of princes is made but an accessory to a cause; and that there be other bands, that tie faster than the band of sovereignty, kings begin to be put almost out of possession.

Also, when discords and quarrels and factions are carried openly, and audaciously; it is a sign, the reverence of government is lost. For the motions of the greatest persons in a government, ought to be, as the motions of the planets, under *primum mobile*; according to the old opinion: which is, that every of them is carried swiftly, by the highest motion, and softly in their own motion. And therefore, when great ones, in their own particular motion, move violently, and, as Tacitus expresseth it well, *liberius quam ut imperantium meminissent*; it is a sign, the orbs are out of frame. For reverence is that, wherewith princes are girt from God; who threatneth the dissolving thereof; *solvam cingula regum*.

So when any of the four pillars of government are mainly shaken, or weakened (which are religion, justice, counsel, and treasure), men had need to pray for fair weather. But let us pass from this part of predictions (concerning which, nevertheless, more light may be taken, from that which followeth); and let us speak first of the materials of seditions; then of the motives of them; and thirdly of the remedies.

Concerning the materials of seditions. It is a thing well to be considered: for the surest way to prevent seditions (if the times do bear it), is to take away the matter of them. For if there be fuel prepared, it is hard to tell, whence the spark shall come, that shall set it on fire. The matter of seditions is of two kinds; much poverty, and much discontentment. It is certain, so many overthrown estates, so many votes for troubles. Lucan noteth well the state of Rome, before the civil war.

> *Hinc usura vorax, rapidumque in tempore foenus,*
> *hinc concussa fides, et multis utile bellum.*

This same *multis utile bellum* is an assured and infallible sign of a state disposed to seditions and troubles. And if this poverty and broken estate, in the better sort, be joined with a want and necessity, in the mean people, the danger is imminent, and great. For the rebellions of the belly are the worst. As for discontentments, they are in the politic body, like to humours in the natural, which are apt to gather a preternatural heat, and to inflame. And let no prince measure the danger of them, by this; whether they be just, or unjust. For that were to imagine people to be too reasonable; who do often spurn at their own good: nor yet by this; whether the griefs, whereupon they rise, be in fact, great or small: for they are the most dangerous discontentments, where the fear is greater than the feeling. *Dolendi modus, timendi non item*. Besides, in great oppressions, the same things that provoke the patience, do withal mate the courage: but in fears it is not so. Neither let any prince, or state, be secure concerning discontentments, because they have been often, or have been long and yet no peril hath ensued; for as it is true, that every vapour, or fume, doth not turn into a storm; so it is, nevertheless, true, that storms, though they blow over divers times, yet may fall at last; and as the Spanish proverb noteth well; The cord breaketh at the last by the weakest pull.

The causes and motives of seditions are; innovation in religion; taxes; alteration of laws and customs; breaking of privileges; general oppression; advancement of unworthy persons; strangers; dearths; disbanded soldiers; factions grown desperate; and whatsoever in offending people, joineth and knitteth them, in a common cause.

For the remedies; there may be some general preservatives, whereof we will speak; as for the just cure, it must answer to the particular disease: and so be left to counsel, rather than rule.

The first remedy or prevention, is to remove by all means possible, that material cause of sedition, whereof we spoke; which is want and poverty in the estate. To which purpose, serveth the opening and well balancing of trade; the cherishing of manufactures; the banishing of idleness; the repressing of waste and excess by sumptuary laws; the improvement and husbanding of the soil; the regulating of prices of things vendible; the moderating of taxes and tributes; and the like. Generally, it is to be foreseen, that the population of a kingdom, (especially if it be not mown down by wars) do not exceed the stock of the kingdom, which should maintain them. Neither is the population to be reckoned only by number: for a smaller number, that spend more, and earn less, do wear out an estate sooner than a greater number, that live lower, and gather more. Therefore the multiplying of nobility, and other degrees of quality, in an over proportion to the common people, doth speedily bring a state to necessity: and so doth likewise an overgrown clergy; for they bring nothing to the stock; and in like manner, when more are bred scholars than preferments can take off.

It is likewise to be remembered, that for as much as the increase of any estate must be upon the foreigner (for whatsoever is somewhere gotten, is somewhere lost), there be but three things, which one nation selleth unto another; the commodity nature yieldeth it; the manufacture; and the vecture or carriage. So that if these three wheels go, wealth will flow as in a spring tide. And it cometh many times to pass, that *materiam superabit opus*; that the work, and carriage, is more worth than the material, and enricheth a state more; as is notably seen in the Low Countrymen, who have the best mines, above ground, in the world.

Above all things, good policy is to be used, that the treasure and moneys in a state be not gathered into few hands. For otherwise, a state may have a great stock, and yet starve. And money is like muck, not good except it be spread. This is done, chiefly, by suppressing, or at the least, keeping a strait hand, upon the devouring trades of usury, engrossing, great pasturages, and the like.

For removing discontentments, or at least, the danger of them; there is in every state (as we know) two portions of subjects; the noblesse, and the commonality. When one of these is discontent, the danger is not great; for common people are of slow motion, if they be not excited by the greater sort; and the greater sort are of small strength, except the multitude be apt and ready to move of themselves. Then is the danger, when the greater sort do but wait for the troubling of the waters, amongst the meaner, that then they may declare themselves. The poets feign, that the rest of the gods would have bound Jupiter; which he hearing of, by the counsel of Pallas, sent for Briareus, with his hundred hands, to come in to his aid. An emblem, no doubt, to show how safe it is for monarchs to make sure of the good will of common people.

To give moderate liberty for griefs and discontentments to evaporate (so it be without too great insolency or bravery) is a safe way. For he that turneth the humours back, and maketh the wound bleed inwards, endangereth malign ulcers, and pernicious impostumations.

The part of Epimetheus mought well become Prometheus, in the case of discontentments; for there is not a better provision against them. Epimetheus, when griefs and evils flew abroad, at last shut the lid, and kept hope in the bottom of the vessel. Certainly, the politic and artificial nourishing and entertaining of hopes, and carrying men from hopes to hopes, is one of the best antidotes against the poison of discontentments. And it is a certain sign of a wise government, and proceeding, when it can hold men's hearts by hopes, when it cannot by satisfaction: and when it can handle things in such manner as no evil shall appear so peremptory, but that it hath some outlet of hope: which is the less hard to do, because both particular persons, and factions, are apt enough to flatter themselves, or at least to brave that, which they believe not.

Also, the foresight, and prevention, that there be no likely or fit head, whereunto discontented persons may resort, and under whom they may join, is a known, but an excellent point of caution. I understand a fit head, to be one that hath greatness, and reputation; that hath confidence with the discontented party; and upon whom they turn their eyes; and that is thought discontented in his own particular; which kind of persons are either to be won, and reconciled to the state, and that in a fast and true manner; or to be fronted, with some other of the same party, that may oppose them, and so divide the reputation. Generally, the dividing and breaking of all factions and combinations that are adverse to the state, and setting them at distance, or at least distrust amongst themselves, is not one of the worst remedies. For it is a desperate case, if those that hold with the proceeding of the state, be full of discord and faction; and those that are against it, be entire and united.

I have noted, that some witty and sharp speeches, which have fallen from princes, have given fire to seditions. Caesar did himself infinite hurt, in that speech; *Sulla nescivit literas, non potuit dictare*: for it did, utterly cut off that hope, which men had entertained, that he would, at one time or other, give over his dictatorship. Galba undid himself by that speech; *legi a se militem, non emi*: for it put the soldiers out of hope of the donative. Probus likewise, by that speech; *si vixero, non opus erit amplius Romano imperio militibus*. A speech of great despair, for the soldiers: and many the like. Surely, princes had need, in tender matters, and ticklish times, to beware what they say; especially in these short speeches, which flee abroad like darts, and are thought to be shot out of their secret intentions. For as for large discourses, they are flat things, and not so much noted.

Lastly, let princes, against all events, not be without some great person, one, or rather more, of military valour near unto them, for the repressing of seditions in their beginnings. For without that, there useth to be more trepidation in court, upon the first breaking out of troubles, than were fit. And the state runneth the danger of that, which Tacitus saith; *atque is habitus animorum fuit, ut pessimum facinus auderent pauci, plures vellent, omnes paterentur*. But let such military persons be assured, and well reputed of, rather then factious, and popular; holding also good correspondence with the other great men in the state; or else the remedy is worse than the disease.

16

Of Atheism

I had rather believe all the fables in the Legend, and the Talmud, and the Alcoran, than that this universal frame is without a mind. And therefore, God never wrought miracle to convince atheism, because his ordinary works convince it. It is true, that a little philosophy inclineth man's mind to atheism; but depth in philosophy bringeth men's minds about to religion: for while the mind of man looketh upon second causes scattered, it may sometimes rest in them, and go no further: but when it beholdeth the chain of them, confederate and linked together, it must needs fly to providence, and deity. Nay, even that school which is most accused of atheism, doth most demonstrate religion; that is, the school of Leucippus, and Democritus, and Epicurus. For it is a thousand times more credible, that four mutable elements, and one immutable fifth essence, duly and eternally placed, needs no God, than that an army of infinite small proportions, or seeds unplaced, should have produced this order, and beauty, without a divine marshal. The scripture saith; The fool hath said in his heart, there is no God: it is not said; The fool hath thought in his heart: so as, he rather saith it by rote to himself, as that he would have, than that he can thoroughly believe it, or be persuaded of it. For none deny there is a God, but those, for whom it maketh that there were no God. It appeareth in nothing more, that atheism is rather in the lip, than in the heart of man, than by this; that atheists will ever be talking of that their opinion, as if they fainted in it, within themselves, and would be glad to be strengthened, by the consent of others: nay more, you shall have atheists strive to get disciples, as it fareth with other sects: and, which is most of all, you shall have of them, that will suffer for atheism, and not recant; whereas, if they did truly think, that there were no such thing as God, why should they trouble themselves? Epicurus is charged, that he did but dissemble, for his credit's sake, when he affirmed, there were blessed natures, but such as enjoyed themselves, without having respect to the government of the world. Wherein, they say, he did temporise; though in secret, he thought, there was no God. But certainly, he is traduced; for his words are noble and divine: *non deos vulgi negare profanum, sed vulgi opiniones diis applicare profanum.* Plato could have said no more. And although he had the confidence to deny the administration, he had not the power to deny the nature. The Indians of the West have names for their particular gods, though they have no name for God: as if the heathens should have had the names Jupiter, Apollo, Mars, &c., but not the word *deus*: which shows, that even those barbarous people have the notion, though they have not the latitude, and extent of it. So that against atheists, the very savages take part, with the very subtlest philosophers. The contemplative atheist is rare; a Diagoras, a Bion, a Lucian perhaps, and some others; and yet they seem to be more than they are; for that, all that impugn a received religion, or superstition, are by the adverse part branded with the name of atheists. But the great atheists, indeed, are hypocrites; which are ever handling holy things, but without feeling. So as they must needs be cauterised in the end. The causes of atheism are; divisions in religion, if they be many; for any one main division addeth zeal to both sides; but many divisions introduce atheism. Another is, scandal of priests; when it is come to that, which St Bernard saith; *non est iam dicere, ut populus, sic sacerdos: quia nec sic populus, ut sacerdos.* A third is, custom of profane scoffing in holy matters; which doth, by little and little, deface the reverence of religion. And lastly, learned times, specially with peace, and prosperity: for troubles and adversities do more bow men's minds to religion. They that deny a God, destroy man's nobility; for certainly, man is of kin to the beasts, by his body; and if he be not of kin to God, by his spirit, he is a base and ignoble creature. It destroys likewise magnanimity, and the raising of human nature: for take an example of a dog; and mark what a generosity and courage he will put on, when he finds himself maintained by a man; who to him is in stead of a God, or *melior natura*: which courage is manifestly such as that creature, without that confidence of a better nature than his own, could never attain. So man, when he resteth and assureth himself upon divine protection, and favour, gathereth a force and faith; which human nature, in itself, could not obtain. Therefore, as atheism is in all respects hateful, so in this, that it depriveth human nature of the means to exalt itself, above human frailty. As it is in particular persons, so it is in nations: never was there such a state, for magnanimity, as Rome: of this state hear what Cicero saith; *Quam volumus licet, patres conscripti, nos amemus, tamen nec numero Hispanos, nec robore Gallos, nec calliditate Poenos, nec artibus Graecos, nec denique hoc ipso huius gentis et terrae domestico nativoque sensu Italos ipsos et Latinos; sed pietate, ac religione, atque hac una sapientia, quod deorum immortalium numine omnia regi gubernarique perspeximus, omnes gentes nationesque superavimus.*

17

Of Superstition

It were better to have no opinion of God at all, than such an opinion, as is unworthy of him: for the one is unbelief, the other is contumely: and certainly superstition is the reproach of the deity. Plutarch saith well to that purpose: Surely (saith he) I had rather, a great deal, men should say, there was no such man at all as Plutarch; than that they should say, that there was one Plutarch, that would eat his children, as soon as they were born, as the poets speak of Saturn. And, as the contumely is greater towards God, so the danger is greater towards men. Atheism leaves a man to sense; to philosophy; to natural piety; to laws; to reputation; all which may be guides to an outward moral virtue, though religion were not; but superstition dismounts all these, and erecteth an absolute monarchy in the minds of men. Therefore atheism did never perturb states; for it makes men wary of themselves, as looking no further: and we see the times inclined to atheism (as the time of Augustus Caesar) were civil times. But superstition hath been the conclusion of many states; and bringeth in a new *primum mobile*, that ravisheth all the spheres of government. The master of superstition is the people; and in all superstition, wise men follow fools; and arguments are fitted to practice, in a reversed order. It was gravely said, by some of the prelates, in the Council of Trent, where the doctrine of the schoolmen bare great sway; that the schoolmen were like astronomers, which did feign eccentrics and epicycles, and such engines of orbs, to save the phenomena; though they knew, there were no such things: and, in like manner, that the schoolmen had framed a number of subtle and intricate axioms, and theorems, to save the practice of the Church. The causes of superstition are: pleasing and sensual rites and ceremonies; excess of outward and pharisaical holiness; over-great reverence of traditions, which cannot but load the Church; the stratagems of prelates for their own ambition and lucre; the favouring too much of good intentions, which openeth the gate to conceits and novelties; the taking an aim at divine matters by human, which cannot but breed mixture of imaginations; and lastly, barbarous times, especially joined with calamities and disasters. Superstition, without a veil, is a deformed thing; for, as it addeth deformity to an ape, to be so like a man; so the similitude of superstition to religion, makes it the more deformed. And as wholesome meat corrupteth to little worms, so good forms and orders corrupt into a number of petty observances. There is a superstition, in avoiding superstition; when men think to do best, if they go furthest from the superstition formerly received: therefore, care would be had, that (as it fareth in ill purgings) the good be not taken away with the bad; which commonly is done, when the people is the reformer.

18

Of Travel

Travel, in the younger sort, is a part of education; in the elder, a part of experience. He that travelleth into a country, before he hath some entrance into the language, goeth to school, and not to travel. That young men travel under some tutor, or grave servant, I allow well; so that he be such a one, that hath the language, and hath been in the country before; whereby he may be able to tell them, what things are worthy to be seen in the country where they go; what acquaintances they are to seek; what exercises or discipline the place yieldeth. For else young men shall go hooded, and look abroad little. It is a strange thing, that in sea voyages, where there is nothing to be seen but sky and sea, men should make diaries; but in land-travel, wherein so much is to be obscured, for the most part, they omit it; as if chance were fitter to be registered than observation. Let diaries, therefore, be brought in use. The things to be seen and observed are: the courts of princes, specially when they give audience to ambassadors: the courts of justice, while they sit and hear causes; and so of consistories ecclesiastics: the churches, and monasteries, with the monuments which are therein extant: the walls and fortifications of cities and towns; and so the havens and harbours: antiquities, and ruins: libraries; colleges, disputations, and lectures, where any are: shipping and navies: houses, and gardens of state and pleasure, near great cities: armories: arsenals: magazines: exchanges: bourses; warehouses: exercises of horsemanship; fencing; training of soldiers; and the like: comedies; such whereunto the better sort of persons do resort; treasuries of jewels, and robes; cabinets, and rarities: and to conclude, whatsoever is memorable in the places where they go. After all which, the tutors or servants ought to make diligent enquiry. As for triumphs; masques; feasts; weddings; funerals; capital executions; and such shows; men need not to be put in mind of them; yet are they not to be neglected. If you will have a young man, to put his travel into a little room, and in short time, to gather much, this you must do. First, as was said, he must have some entrance into the language, before he goeth. Then he must have such a servant, or tutor, as knoweth the country, as was likewise said. Let him carry with him also some card or book describing the country, where he travelleth; which will be a good key to his enquiry. Let him keep also a diary. Let him not stay long in one city, or town; more or less as the place deserveth, but not long: nay, when he stayeth in one city or town, let him change his lodging, from one end and part of the town to another; which is a great adamant of acquaintance. Let him sequester himself from the company of his countrymen, and diet in such places, where there is good company of the nation where he travelleth. Let him upon his removes, from one place to another, procure recommendation to some person of quality, residing in the place whither he removeth; that he may use his favour in those things he desireth to see or know. Thus he may abridge his travel, with much profit. As for the acquaintance, which is to be sought in travel; that which is most of all profitable, is acquaintance with the secretaries and employed men of ambassadors; for so in travelling in one country he shall suck the experience of many. Let him also see and visit imminent persons, in all kinds, which are of great fame abroad; that he may be able to tell, how the life agreeth with the same. For quarrels, they are with care and discretion to be avoided: they are, commonly, for mistresses; healths; place; and words. And let a man beware, how he keepeth company with choleric and quarrelsome persons; for they will engage him into their own quarrels. When a traveller returneth home, let him not leave the countries where he hath travelled altogether behind him; but maintain a correspondence, by letters, with those of his acquaintance, which are of most worth. And let his travel appear rather in his discourse, than in his apparel, or gesture: and in his discourse, let him be rather advised in his answers, then forwards to tell stories: and let it appear, that he doth not change his country manners for those of foreign parts; but only prick in some flowers, of that he hath learned abroad, into the customs of his own country.

19

Of Empire

It is a miserable state of mind, to have few things to desire, and many things to fear: and yet that commonly is the case of kings; who being at the highest, want matter of desire, which makes their minds more languishing; and have many representations of perils and shadows, which makes their minds the less clear. And this is one reason also of that effect, which the scripture speaketh of; that the king's heart is inscrutable. For multitude of jealousies, and lack of some predominant desire, that should marshal and put in order all the rest, maketh any man's heart hard to find, or sound. Hence it comes likewise, that princes, many times, make themselves desires, and set their hearts upon toys: sometimes upon a building; sometimes upon erecting of an order; sometimes upon the advancing of a person; sometimes upon obtaining excellency in some art, or feat of the hand; as Nero for playing on the harp, Domitian for certainty of the hand with the arrow, Commodus for playing at fence, Caracalla for driving chariots, and the like. This seemeth incredible unto those that know not the principle; that the mind of man is more cheered, and refreshed, by profiting in small things, than by standing at a stay in great. We see also that kings, that have been fortunate conquerors in their first years; it being not possible for them to go forward infinitely, but that they must have some check or arrest in their fortunes; turn in their latter years to be superstitious and melancholy: as did Alexander the Great; Dioclesian; and in our memory, Charles the Fifth; and others: for he that is used to go forward, and findeth a stop, falleth out of his own favour, and is not the thing he was.

To speak now of the true temper of empire: it is a thing rare, and hard to keep: for both temper and distemper consist of contraries. But it is one thing to mingle contraries, another to interchange them. The answer of Apollonius to Vespasian is full of excellent instruction; Vespasian asked him; What was Nero's overthrow? He answered; Nero could touch and tune the harp well; but in government, sometimes he used to wind the pins too high, sometimes to let them down too low. And certain it is, that nothing destroyeth authority so much, as the unequal and untimely interchange of power pressed too far, and relaxed too much.

This is true; that the wisdom of all these latter times in princes' affairs, is rather fine deliveries, and shiftings of dangers and mischiefs, when they are near, than solid and grounded courses to keep them aloof. But this is but to try masteries with fortune: and let men beware, how they neglect, and suffer matter of trouble to be prepared: for no man can forbid the spark, nor tell whence it may come. The difficulties in princes' business are many and great; but the greatest difficulty, is often in their own mind. For it is common with princes (saith Tacitus) to will contradictories. *Sunt plerumque regum voluntates vehementes et inter se contrariae*. For it is the solecism of power, to think to command the end, and yet not to endure the mean.

Kings have to deal with their neighbours; their wives; their children; their prelates or clergy; their nobles; their second-nobles or gentlemen; their merchants; their commons; and their men of war; and from all these arise dangers, if care and circumspection be not used.

First for their neighbours; there can no general rule be given (the occasions are so variable), save one; which ever holdeth; which is, that princes do keep due sentinel, that none of their neighbours do overgrow so (by increase of territory, by embracing of trade, by approaches, or the like), as they become more able to annoy them, than they were. And this is, generally, the work of standing councils to foresee, and to hinder it. During that triumvirate of kings, King Henry VIII of England, Francis I, King of France, and Charles V, Emperor, there was such a watch kept, that none of the three could win a palm of ground, but the other two would straightways balance it, either by confederation, or, if need were, by a war: and would not, in any wise, take up peace at interest. And the like was done by that league (which, Guicciardine saith, was the security of Italy) made between Ferdinando King of Naples; Lorenzius Medices, and Ludovicus Sforza, potentates, the one of Florence, the other of Milan. Neither is the opinion of some of the schoolmen to be received; that a war cannot justly be made, but upon a precedent injury, or provocation. For there is no question, but a just fear of an imminent danger, though there be no blow given, is a lawful cause of a war.

For their wives; there are cruel examples of them. Livia is enfamed for the poisoning of her husband: Roxolana, Solyman's wife, was the destruction of that renowned prince, Sultan Mustapha; and otherwise troubled his house, and succession: Edward the Second of England his queen had the principal hand, in the deposing and murder of her husband. This kind of danger is then to be feared, chiefly, when the wives have plots for the raising of their own children; or else that they be adulteresses.

For their children: the tragedies, likewise, of dangers from them, have been many. And generally, the entering of fathers into suspicion of their children, hath been ever unfortunate. The destruction of Mustapha (that we named before) was so fatal to Solyman's line, as the succession of the Turks, from Solyman, until this day, is suspected to be untrue, and of strange blood; for that Selymus the Second was thought to be supposititious. The destruction of Crispus, a young prince of rare towardness, by Constantinus the Great, his father, was in like manner fatal to his house; for both Constantinus, and Constance, his sons, died violent deaths; and Constantius, his other son, did little better; who died, indeed, of sickness, but after that Julianus had taken arms against him. The destruction of Demetrius, son to Philip the Second, of Macedonia, turned upon the father, who died of repentance. And many like examples there are: but few, or none, where the fathers had good by such distrust; except it were, where the sons were up in open arms against them; as was Selymus the First against Baiazet: and the three sons of Henry the Second, King of England.

For their prelates; when they are proud and great, there is also danger from them: as it was, in the times of Anselmus, and Thomas Becket, Archbishops of Canterbury; who with their croziers, did almost try it, with the king's sword; and yet they had to deal with stout and haughty kings; William Rufus, Henry the First, and Henry the Second. The danger is not from that state, but where it hath a dependence of foreign authority; or where the churchmen come in, and are elected, not by the collation of the king, or particular patrons, but by the people.

For their nobles; to keep them at a distance, it is not amiss; but to depress them, may make a king more absolute, but less safe; and less able to perform anything that he desires. I have noted it, in my history of King Henry the Seventh of England, who depressed his nobility; whereupon, it came to pass that his times were full of difficulties, and troubles; for the nobility, though they continued loyal unto him, yet did they not cooperate with him in his business. So that in effect, he was fain to do all things, himself.

For their second nobles; there is not much danger from them, being a body dispersed. They may sometimes discourse high, but that doth little hurt: besides, they are a counterpoise to the higher nobility, that they grow not too potent: and lastly, being the most immediate in authority, with the common people, they do best temper popular commotions.

For their merchants; they are *vena porta*; and if they flourish not, a kingdom may have good limbs, but will have empty veins, and nourish little. Taxes, and imposts upon them, do seldom good to the king's revenue; for that that he wins in the hundred, he loseth in the shire; the particular rates being increased, but the total bulk of trading rather decreased.

For their commons; there is little danger from them, except it be, where they have great and potent heads; or where you meddle with the point of religion; or their customs, or means of life.

For their men of war; it is a dangerous state, where they live and remain in a body, and are used to donatives; whereof we see examples in the Janissaries, and Pretorian bands of Rome: but trainings of men, and arming them in several places, and under several commanders, and without donatives, are things of defence, and no danger.

Princes are like to heavenly bodies, which cause good or evil times; and which have much veneration, but no rest. All precepts concerning kings, are in effect comprehended in those two remembrances: *memento quod es homo*; and *memento quod es deus*, or *vice dei*: the one bridleth their power, and the other their will.

20

Of Counsel

The greatest trust between man and man is the trust of giving counsel. For in other confidences, men commit the parts of life; their lands, their goods, their children, their credit, some particular affair; but to such as they make their counsellors they commit the whole: by how much the more, they are obliged to all faith and integrity. The wisest princes need not think it any diminution to their greatness, or derogation to their sufficiency, to rely upon counsel. God himself is not without: but hath made it one of the great names of his blessed son; the counsellor. Solomon hath pronounced, that in counsel is stability. Things will have their first or second agitation; if they be not tossed upon the arguments of counsel they will be tossed upon the waves of fortune; and be full of inconstancy, doing, and undoing, like the reeling of a drunken man. Solomon's son found the force of counsel as his father saw the necessity of it. For the beloved kingdom of God was first rent and broken by ill counsel; upon which counsel there are set, for our instruction, the two marks, whereby bad counsel is for ever best discerned: that it was young counsel for the persons; and violent counsel for the matter.

The ancient times do set forth in figure both the incorporation and inseparable conjunction of counsel with kings; and the wise and politic use of counsel by kings: the one, in that they say, Jupiter did marry Metis, which signifieth counsel: whereby they intend, that sovereignty is married to counsel: the other, in that which followeth, which was thus: they say after Jupiter was married to Metis, she conceived by him, and was with child; but Jupiter suffered her not to stay till she brought forth, but ate her up; whereby he became himself with child, and was delivered of Pallas armed, out of his head. Which monstrous fable containeth a secret of empire; how kings are to make use of their counsel of state. That first, they ought to refer matters unto them, which is the first begetting or impregnation; but when they are elaborate, moulded, and shaped, in the womb of their counsel, and grow ripe, and ready to be brought forth; that then, they suffer not their counsel to go through with the resolution, and direction, as if it depended on them; but take the matter back into their own hands, and make it appear to the world, that the decrees, and final directions (which, because they come forth with prudence, and power, are resembled to Pallas armed) proceeded from themselves: and not only from their authority, but (the more to add reputation to themselves) from their head, and device.

Let us now speak of the inconveniences of counsel, and of the remedies. The inconveniences, that have been noted in calling and using counsel, are three. First, the revealing of affairs, whereby they become less secret. Secondly, the weakening of the authority of princes, as if they were less of themselves. Thirdly, the danger of being unfaithfully counselled, and more for the good of them that counsel, than of him that is counselled. For which inconveniences, the doctrine of Italy, and practice of France, in some kings' times, hath introduced cabinet counsels; a remedy worse then the disease.

As to secrecy; princes are not bound to communicate all matters with all counsellors; but may extract and select. Neither is it necessary, that he that consulteth what he should do, should declare what he will do. But let princes beware, that the unsecreting of their affairs comes not from themselves. And as for cabinet counsels, it may be their motto; *plenus rimarum sum*: one futile person, that maketh it his glory to tell, will do more hurt than many, that know it their duty to conceal. It is true, there be some affairs, which require extreme secrecy, which will hardly go beyond one or two persons, besides the king: neither are those counsels unprosperous: for besides the secrecy, they commonly go on constantly in one spirit of direction, without distraction. But then it must be a prudent king, such as is able to grind with a hand-mill; and those inward counsellors had need also be wise men, and especially true and trusty to the king's ends; as it was with King Henry the Seventh of England, who in his greatest business imparted himself to none, except it were to Morton, and Fox.

For weakening of authority; the fable showeth the remedy. Nay, the majesty of kings is rather exalted, than diminished, when they are in the chair of counsel: neither was there ever prince bereaved of his dependencies by his counsel; except where there hath been, either an overgreatness in one counsellor, or an overstrict combination in divers; which are things soon found, and holpen.

For the last inconvenience, that men will counsel with an eye to themselves; certainly, *non inveniet fidem super terram*, is meant of the nature of times, and not of all particular persons; there be, that are in nature faithful, and sincere, and plain, and direct; not crafty, and involved: let princes, above all, draw to themselves such natures. Besides, counsellors are not commonly so united, but that one counsellor keepeth sentinel over another; so that if any do counsel out of faction, or private ends, it commonly comes to the king's ear. But the best remedy is, if princes know their counsellors, as well as their counsellors know them:

principis est virtus maxima nosse suos.

And on the other side, counsellors should not be too speculative into their sovereign's person. The true composition of a counsellor, is rather to be skilful in their master's business, than in his nature; for then he is like to advise him, and not to feed his humour. It is of singular use to princes, if they take the opinions of their counsel both separately and together. For private opinion is more free; but opinion before others is more reverend. In private, men are more bold in their own humours; and in consort, men are more obnoxious to others' humours; therefore it is good to take both: and of the inferior sort, rather in private, to preserve freedom; of the greater, rather in consort, to preserve respect. It is in vain for princes to take counsel concerning matters, if they take no counsel likewise concerning persons: for all matters, are as dead images; and the life of the execution of affairs resteth in the good choice of persons. Neither is it enough to consult concerning persons, *secundum genera*, as in an idea, or mathematical description, what the kind and character of the person should be; for the greatest errors are committed, and the most judgement is shown, in the choice of individuals. It was truly said; *optimi consiliarii mortui*; books will speak plain, when counsellors blanch. Therefore it is good to be conversant in them; specially the books of such as themselves have been actors upon the stage.

The counsels, at this day, in most places are but familiar meetings; where matters are rather talked on, than debated. And they run too swift to the order or act of counsel. It were better, that in causes of weight, the matter were propounded one day, and not spoken to, till the next day; *in nocte consilium.* So was it done, in the commission of union between England and Scotland; which was a grave and orderly assembly. I commend set days for petitions: for both it gives the suitors more certainty for their attendance; and it frees the meetings for matters of estate, that they may *hoc agere.* In choice of committees, for ripening business for the counsel, it is better to choose indifferent persons, than to make an indifference, by putting in those that are strong on both sides. I commend also standing commissions; as for trade; for treasure; for war; for suits; for some provinces: for where there be divers particular counsels, and but one counsel of estate (as it is in Spain), they are in effect no more than standing commissions; save that they have greater authority. Let such as are to inform counsels, out of their particular professions (as lawyers, seamen, mintmen, and the like), be first heard before committees; and then, as occasion serves, before the counsel. And let them not come in multitudes, or in a tribunitious manner; for that is to clamour counsels, not to inform them. A long table, and a square table, or seats about the walls, seem things of form, but are things of substance; for at a long table, a few at the upper end, in effect, sway all the business; but in the other form, there is more use of the counsellors' opinions, that sit lower. A king, when he presides in counsel, let him beware how he opens his own inclination too much, in that which he propoundeth: for else counsellors will but take the wind of him; and instead of giving free counsel, sing him a song of *placebo.*

21

Of Delays

Fortune is like the market; where many times, if you can stay a little, the price will fall. And again, it is sometimes like Sybilla's offer; which at first offereth the commodity at full, then consumeth part and part, and still holdeth up the price. For occasion (as it is in the common verse) turneth a bald noddle, after he hath presented her locks in front, and no hold taken: or at least turneth the handle of the bottle, first to be received, and after the belly, which is hard to clasp. There is surely no greater wisdom, then well to time the beginnings and onsets of things. Dangers are no more light, if they once seem light: and more dangers have deceived men, than forced them. Nay, it were better, to meet some dangers half way, though they come nothing near, than to keep too long a watch upon their approaches; for if a man watch too long, it is odds he will fall asleep. On the other side, to be deceived, with too long shadows (as some have been, when the moon was low, and shone on their enemies back), and so to shoot off before the time; or to teach dangers to come on, by over early buckling towards them, is another extreme. The ripeness, or unripeness of the occasion (as we said) must ever be well weighed; and generally, it is good, to commit the beginnings of all great actions to Argos with his hundred eyes; and the ends to Briareus with his hundred hands: first to watch, and then to speed. For the helmet of Pluto, which maketh the politic man go invisible, is secrecy in the counsel, and celerity in the execution. For when things are once come to the execution, there is no secrecy comparable to celerity; like the motion of a bullet in the air, which flieth so swift, as it outruns the eye.

22

Of Cunning

We take cunning for a sinister or crooked wisdom. And certainly, there is great difference, between a cunning man, and a wise man; not only in point of honesty, but in point of ability. There be that can pack the cards, and yet cannot play well; so there are some, that are good in canvasses, and factions, that are otherwise weak men. Again, it is one thing to understand persons, and another thing to understand matters; for many are perfect in men's humours, that are not greatly capable of the real part of business; which is the constitution of one that hath studied men, more than books. Such men are fitter for practice, than for counsel; and they are good but in their own alley: turn them to new men, and they have lost their aim; so as the old rule, to know a fool from a wise man; *mitte ambos nudos ad ignotos, et videbis*; doth scarce hold for them. And because these cunning men are like haberdashers of small wares, it is not amiss to set forth their shop.

It is a point of cunning to wait upon him, with whom you speak, with your eye; as the Jesuits give it in precept: for there be many wise men, that have secret hearts, and transparent countenances. Yet this would be done with a demure abasing of your eye sometimes, as the Jesuits also do use.

Another is, that when you have anything to obtain of present dispatch, you entertain and amuse the party, with whom you deal, with some other discourse; that he be not too much awake, to make objections. I knew a counsellor and secretary, that never came to Queen Elizabeth of England, with bills to sign, but he would always first put her into some discourse of estate, that she mought the less mind the bills.

The like surprise may be made, by moving things, when the party is in haste, and cannot stay to consider advisedly of that is moved.

If a man would cross a business, that he doubts some other would handsomely and effectually move, let him pretend to wish it well, and move it himself, in such sort, as may foil it.

The breaking off, in the midst of that one was about to say, as if he took himself up, breeds a greater appetite in him, with whom you confer, to know more.

And because it works better, when anything seemeth to be gotten from you by question, than if you offer it of yourself, you may lay a bait for a question, by showing another visage and countenance than you are wont; to the end, to give occasion, for the party to ask, what the matter is of the change? As Nehemias did; And I had not before that time been sad before the king.

In things, that are tender and unpleasing, it is good to break the ice by some whose words are of less weight, and to reserve the more weighty voice to come in, as by chance, so that he may be asked the question upon the other's speech. As Narcissus did, in relating to Claudius the marriage of Messalina and Silius.

In things, that a man would not be seen in himself; it is a point of cunning, to borrow the name of the world; as to say; The world says, or, There is a speech abroad.

I knew one, that when he wrote a letter, he would put that which was most material, in the post-script, as if it had been a by-matter.

I knew another, that when he came to have speech, he would pass over that that he intended most, and go forth, and come back again, and speak of it, as of a thing that he had almost forgot.

Some procure themselves to be surprised, at such times as it is like, the party that they work upon, will suddenly come upon them; and to be found with a letter in their hand, or doing somewhat which they are not accustomed; to the end, they may be apposed of those things, which of themselves they are desirous to utter.

It is a point of cunning, to let fall those words, in a man's own name, which he would have another man learn, and use, and thereupon take advantage. I knew two, that were competitors, for the secretary's place, in Queen Elizabeth's time, and yet kept good quarter between themselves: and would confer, one with another, upon the business; and the one of them said, that to be a secretary, in the declination of a monarchy, was a ticklish thing, and that he did not affect it: the other, straight caught up those words, and discoursed with divers of his friends, that he had no reason to desire to be secretary, in the declination of a monarchy. The first man took hold of it, and found means, it was told the queen; who hearing of a declination of a monarchy, took it so ill, as she would never after hear of the other's suit.

There is a cunning, which we in England call the turning of the cat in the pan; which is, when that which a man says to another, he lays it, as if another had said it to him. And to say truth, it is not easy, when such a matter passed between two, to make it appear, from which of them it first moved and began.

It is a way that some men have, to glance and dart at others, by justifying themselves, by negatives; as to say, this do not: as Tigellinus did towards Burrus; *se non diversas spes, sed incolumitatem imperatoris simpliciter spectare.*

Some have in readiness so many tales and stories, as there is nothing they would insinuate but they can wrap it into a tale; which serveth both to keep themselves more in guard, and to make others carry it, with more pleasure.

It is a good point of cunning, for a man to shape the answer he would have, in his own words, and propositions; for it makes the other party stick the less.

It is strange, how long some men will lie in wait, to speak somewhat they desire to say; and how far about they will fetch; and how many other matters they will beat over, to come near it. It is a thing of great patience, but yet of much use.

A sudden, bold, and unexpected question, doth many times surprise a man, and lay him open. Like to him, that having changed his name, and walking in Paul's, another suddenly came behind him, and called him by his true name, whereat straightways he looked back.

But these small wares, and petty points of cunning, are infinite: and it were a good deed to make a list of them: for that nothing doth more hurt in a state, than that cunning men pass for wise.

But certainly, some there are, that know the resorts and falls of business, that cannot sink into the main of it: like a house, that hath convenient stairs, and entries, but never a fair room. Therefore, you shall see them find out pretty looses in the conclusion, but are no ways able to examine, or debate matters. And yet commonly they take advantage of their inability, and would be thought wits of direction. Some build rather upon the abusing of others, and (as we now say) putting tricks upon them, than upon soundness of their own proceedings. But Solomon saith; *prudens advertit ad gressus suos: stultus divertit ad dolos.*

23

Of Wisdom for a Man's Self

An ant is a wise creature for itself; but it is a shrewd thing, in an orchard, or garden. And certainly, men that are great lovers of themselves, waste the public. Divide with reason between self-love, and society: and be so true to thy self, as thou be not false to others; specially to thy king, and country. It is a poor centre of a man's actions, himself. It is right earth. For that only stands fast upon his own centre; whereas all things that have affinity with the heavens, move upon the centre of another, which they benefit. The referring of all to a man's self, is more tolerable in a sovereign prince; because themselves are not only themselves; but their good and evil, is at the peril of the public fortune. But it is a desperate evil in a servant to a prince, or a citizen in a republic. For whatsoever affairs pass such a man's hands, he crooketh them to his own ends: which must needs be often eccentric to the ends of his master, or state. Therefore let princes, or states, choose such servants as have not this mark; except they mean their service should be made but the accessory. That which maketh the effect more pernicious, is that all proportion is lost. It were disproportion enough, for the servant's good to be preferred before the master's; but yet it is a greater extreme, when a little good of the servant shall carry things against a great good of the master's. And yet that is the case of bad officers, treasurers, ambassadors, generals, and other false and corrupt servants; which set a bias upon their bowl, of their own petty ends, and envies, to the overthrow of their master's great and important affairs. And for the most part, the good such servants receive is after the model of their own fortune; but the hurt they sell for that good is after the model of their master's fortune. And certainly, it is the nature of extreme self-lovers; as they will set an house on fire, and it were but to roast their eggs: and yet these men, many times, hold credit with their masters, because their study is but to please them, and profit themselves: and for either respect, they will abandon the good of their affairs.

Wisdom for a man's self, is in many branches thereof, a depraved thing. It is the wisdom of rats, that will be sure to leave a house, somewhat before it fall. It is the wisdom of the fox, that thrusts out the badger, who digged and made room for him. It is the wisdom of crocodiles, that shed tears, when they would devour. But that which is specially to be noted is that those which (as Cicero says of Pompey) are *sui amantes sine rivali,* are many times unfortunate. And whereas they have all their time sacrificed to themselves, they become in the end themselves sacrifices to the inconstancy of fortune; whose wings they thought, by their self-wisdom, to have pinioned.

24

Of Innovations

As the births of living creatures, at first, are ill shapen: so are all innovations, which are the births of time. Yet notwithstanding, as those that first bring honour into their family, are commonly more worthy, than most that succeed: so the first precedent (if it be good) is seldom attained by imitation. For ill, to man's nature, as it stands perverted, hath a natural motion, strongest in continuance: but good, as a forced motion, strongest at first. Surely every medicine is an innovation; and he that will not apply new remedies, must expect new evils: for time is the greatest innovator: and if time, of course, alter things to the worse, and wisdom and counsel shall not alter them to the better, what shall be the end? It is true, that what is settled by custom, though it be not good, yet at least it is fit. And those things, which have long gone together, are as it were confederate within themselves: whereas new things piece not so well; but though they help by their utility, yet they trouble by their inconformity. Besides, they are like strangers; more admired, and less favoured. All this is true, if time stood still; which contrariwise moveth so round, that a froward retention of custom is as turbulent a thing as an innovation: and they that reverence too much old times, are but a scorn to the new. It were good therefore, that men in their innovations, would follow the example of time itself; which indeed innovateth greatly, but quietly, and by degrees, scarce to be perceived: for otherwise, whatsoever is new, is unlooked for; and ever it mends some, and pairs other: and he that is holpen, takes it for a fortune, and thanks the time; and he that is hurt, for a wrong, and imputeth it to the author. It is good also, not to try experiments in states, except the necessity be urgent, or the utility evident: and well to beware, that it be the reformation, that draweth on the change; and not the desire of change, that pretendeth the reformation. And lastly, that the novelty, though it be not rejected, yet be held for a suspect: and, as the scripture saith; that we make a stand upon the ancient way, and then look about us, and discover what is the straight and right way, and so to walk in it.

25

Of Dispatch

Affected dispatch is one of the most dangerous things to business that can be. It is like that, which the physicians call predigestion, or hasty digestion; which is sure to fill the body full of crudities, and secret seeds of diseases. Therefore, measure not dispatch by the times of sitting, but by the advancement of the business. And as in races, it is not the large stride, or high lift, that makes the speed: so in business, the keeping close to the matter, and not taking of it too much at once, procureth dispatch. It is the care of some, only to come off speedily for the time; or to contrive some false periods of business, because they may seem men of dispatch. But it is one thing, to abbreviate by contracting, another by cutting off: and business so handled at several sittings or meetings, goeth commonly backward and forward, in an unsteady manner. I knew a wise man, that had it for a by-word, when he saw men hasten to a conclusion; Stay a little, that we may make an end the sooner.

On the other side, true dispatch is a rich thing. For time is the measure of business, as money is of wares: and business is bought at a dear hand, where there is small dispatch. The Spartans, and Spaniards, have been noted to be of small dispatch; *Mi venga la muerta de Spagna*; Let my death come from Spain; for then it will be sure to be long in coming.

Give good hearing to those that give the first information in business; and rather direct them in the beginning, than interrupt them in the continuance of their speeches: for he that is put out of his own order, will go forward and backward, and be more tedious while he waits upon his memory, than he could have been, if he had gone on in his own course. But sometimes it is seen, that the moderator is more troublesome than the actor.

Iterations are commonly loss of time: but there is no such gain of time, as to iterate often the state of the question: for it chaseth away many a frivolous speech, as it is coming forth. Long and curious speeches are as fit for dispatch, as a robe or mantle with a long train, is for race. Prefaces, and passages, and excusations, and other speeches of reference to the person, are great wastes of time; and though they seem to proceed of modesty, they are bravery. Yet beware of being too material, when there is any impediment or obstruction in men's wills; for pre-occupation of mind ever requireth preface of speech; like a fomentation to make the unguent enter.

Above all things, order, and distribution, and singling out of parts, is the life of dispatch; so as the distribution be not too subtle: for he that doth not divide will never enter well into business; and he that divideth too much will never come out of it clearly. To choose time is to save time; and an unseasonable motion is but beating the air. There be three parts of business: the preparation; the debate, or examination; and the perfection. Whereof, if you look for dispatch, let the middle only be the work of many, and the first and last the work of few. The proceeding upon somewhat conceived in writing, doth for the most part facilitate dispatch: for though it should be wholly rejected, yet that negative is more pregnant of direction than an indefinite; as ashes are more generative than dust.

26

Of Seeming Wise

It hath been an opinion, that the French are wiser than they seem; and the Spaniards seem wiser than they are. But howsoever it be between nations, certainly it is so between man and man. For as the apostle saith of godliness; Having a show of godliness, but denying the power thereof; so certainly, there are in points of wisdom, and sufficiency, that do nothing or little, very solemnly; *magno conatu nugas*. It is a ridiculous thing, and fit for a satire, to persons of judgement, to see what shifts these formalists have, and what prospectives, to make superficies to seem body, that hath depth and bulk. Some are so close and reserved, as they will not show their wares, but by a dark light: and seem always to keep back somewhat: and when they know within themselves, they speak of that they do not well know, would nevertheless seem to others, to know of that which they may not well speak. Some help themselves with countenance, and gesture, and are wise by signs; as Cicero saith of Piso, that when he answered him, he fetched one of his brows up to his forehead, and bent the other down to his chin: *respondes, altero ad frontem sublato, altero ad mentum depresso supercilio, crudelitatem tibi non placere*. Some think to bear it, by speaking a great word, and being peremptory; and go on, and take by admittance that which they cannot make good. Some, whatsoever is beyond their recall, will seem to despise or make light of it, as impertinent, or curious; and so would have their ignorance seem judgement. Some are never without a difference, and commonly by amusing men with a subtlety, blanch the matter; of whom A. Gellius saith; *hominem delirum, qui verborum minutiis rerum frangit pondera*. Of which kind also, Plato in his *Protagoras* bringeth in Prodicus, in scorn, and maketh him make a speech, that consisteth of distinctions from the beginning to the end.

Generally, such men in all deliberations find ease to be of the negative side, and affect a credit, to object and foretell difficulties: for when propositions are denied, there is an end of them; but if they be allowed, it requireth a new work: which false point of wisdom is the bane of business. To conclude, there is no decaying merchant, or inward beggar, hath so many tricks, to uphold the credit of their wealth, as these empty persons have, to maintain the credit of their sufficiency. Seeming wise men may make shift to get opinion: but let no man choose them for employment; for certainly, you were better take for business a man somewhat absurd than over formal.

27

Of Friendship

It had been hard for him that spake it, to have put more truth and untruth together in few words, than in that speech; Whosoever is delighted in solitude, is either a wild beast, or a god. For it is most true, that a natural and secret hatred, and aversion towards society, in any man, hath somewhat of the savage beast; but it is most untrue, that it should have any character at all of the divine nature; except it proceed, not out of a pleasure in solitude, but out of a love and desire to sequester a man's self, or a higher conversation: such as is found, to have been falsely and feignedly, in some of the heathen; as Epimenides the Candian, Numa the Roman, Empedocles the Sicilian, and Apollonius of Tyana; and truly and really, in divers of the ancient hermits, and holy fathers of the Church. But little do men perceive, what solitude is, and how far it extendeth. For a crowd is not company; and faces are but a gallery of pictures; and talk but a tinkling cymbal, where there is no love. The Latin adage meeteth with it a little; *magna civitas, magna solitudo*; because in a great town, friends are scattered; so that there is not that fellowship, for the most part, which is in less neighbourhoods. But we may go further, and affirm most truly; that it is a mean and miserable solitude, to want true friends; without which the world is but a wilderness: and even in this sense also of solitude, whosoever in the frame of his nature and affections is unfit for friendship, he taketh it of the beast, and not from humanity.

A principal fruit of friendship is the ease and discharge of the fullness and swellings of the heart, which passions of all kinds do cause and induce. We know diseases of stoppings, and suffocations, are the most dangerous in the body; and it is not much otherwise in the mind: you may take sarza to open the liver; steel to open the spleen;

flower of sulphur for the lungs; castoreum for the brain; but no receipt openeth the heart, but a true friend, to whom you may impart griefs, joys, fears, hopes, suspicions, counsels, and whatsoever lieth upon the heart, to oppress it, in a kind of civil shrift or confession.

It is a strange thing to observe how high a rate great kings and monarchs do set upon this fruit of friendship, whereof we spoke: so great, as they purchase it, many times, at the hazard of their own safety, and greatness. For princes, in regard of the distance of their fortune from that of their subjects and servants, cannot gather this fruit, except (to make themselves capable thereof) they raise some persons, to be as it were companions, and almost equals to themselves, which many times sorteth to inconvenience. The modern languages give unto such persons, the name of favourites, or privadoes; as if it were matter of grace, or conversation. But the Roman name attaineth the true use, and cause thereof; naming them *participes curarum*; for it is that which tieth the knot. And we see plainly that this hath been done, not by weak and passionate princes only, but by the wisest, and most politic that ever reigned; who have oftentimes joined to themselves some of their servants; whom both themselves have called friends, and allowed others likewise to call them in the same manner; using the word which is received between private men.

L. Sulla, when he commanded Rome, raised Pompey (after surnamed the Great) to that height, that Pompey vaunted himself for Sulla's overmatch. For when he had carried the consulship for a friend of his, against the pursuit of Sulla, and that Sulla did a little resent thereat, and began to speak great, Pompey turned upon him again, and in effect bade him be quiet; For that more men adored the sun rising, than the sun setting. With Julius Caesar, Decimus Brutus had obtained that interest, as he set him down in his testament, for heir in remainder, after his nephew. And this was the man, that had power with him to draw him forth to his death. For when Caesar would have discharged the senate, in regard of some ill presages, and especially a dream of Calpurnia; this man lifted him gently by the arm, out of his chair, telling him, he hoped he would not dismiss the senate, till his wife had dreamt a better dream. And it seemeth, his favour was so great, as Antonius in a letter which is recited verbatim, in one of Cicero's *Philippics*, calleth him *venefica*, witch; as if he had enchanted Caesar. Augustus raised Agrippa (though of mean birth) to that height, as when he consulted with Maecenas about the marriage of his daughter Julia, Maecenas took the liberty to tell him, that he must either marry his daughter to Agrippa, or take away his life; there was no third way, he had made him so great. With Tiberius Caesar, Seianus had ascended to that height, as they two were termed and reckoned, as a pair of friends. Tiberius in a letter to him saith; *haec pro amicitia nostra non occultavi*: and the whole senate dedicated an altar to friendship, as to a goddess, in respect of the great dearness of friendship between them two. The like or more was between Septimius Severus, and Plautianus. For he forced his eldest son to marry the daughter of Plautianus; and would often maintain Plautianus, in doing affronts to his son: and did write also in a letter to the senate, by these words; I love the man so well, as I wish he may over-live me. Now if these princes had been as a Trajan, or a Marcus Aurelius, a man might have thought, that this had proceeded of an abundant goodness of nature; but being men so wise, of such strength and severity of mind, and so extreme lovers of themselves, as all these were; it proveth most plainly, that they found their own felicity (though as great as ever happened to mortal men) but as an half piece, except they mought have a friend to make it entire: and yet, which is more, they were princes that had wives, sons, nephews; and yet all these could not supply the comfort of friendship.

It is not to be forgotten, what Commineus observeth of his first master Duke Charles the Hardy; namely, that he would communicate his secrets with none; and least of all, those secrets, which troubled him most. Whereupon he goeth on, and saith, that towards his latter time that closeness did impair and a little perish his understanding. Surely Commineus mought have made the same judgement also, if it had pleased him, of his second master Lewis the Eleventh, whose closeness was indeed his tormentor. The parable of Pythagoras is dark, but true; *cor ne edito*; eat not the heart. Certainly, if a man would give it a hard phrase, Those that want friends to open themselves unto, are cannibals of their own hearts. But one thing is most admirable (wherewith I will conclude this first fruit of friendship), which is that this communicating of a man's self to his friend works two contrary effects; for it redoubleth joys, and cutteth griefs in halves. For there is no man, that imparteth his joys to his friend, but he joyeth the more; and no man, that imparteth his griefs to his friend, but he grieveth the less. So that it is, in truth of operation upon a man's mind, of like virtue, as the alchemists use to attribute to their stone, for man's body; that it worketh all contrary effects, but still to the good and benefit of nature. But yet, without praying in aid of alchemists, there is a manifest image of this, in the ordinary course of nature. For in bodies, union strengtheneth and cherisheth any natural action; and, on the other side, weakeneth and dulleth any violent impression: and even so is it of minds.

The second fruit of friendship is healthful and sovereign for the understanding as the first is for the affections. For frendship maketh indeed a fair day in the affections from storm and tempests: but it maketh daylight in the understanding, out of darkness and confusion of thoughts. Neither is this to be understood, only of faithful counsel, which a man receiveth from his friend; but before you come to that, certain it is, that whosoever hath his mind fraught with many thoughts, his wits and understanding do clarify and break up, in the communicating and discoursing with another: he tosseth his thoughts more easily; he marshalleth them more orderly; he seeth how they look when they are turned into words; finally, he waxeth wiser than himself; and that more by an hour's discourse, then by a day's meditation. It was well said by Themistocles to the king of Persia; that speech was like cloth of Arras, opened, and put abroad; whereby the imagery doth appear in figure; whereas in thoughts they lie but as in packs. Neither is this second fruit of friendship, in opening the understanding, restrained only to such friends as are able to give a man counsel: (they indeed are best) but even, without that, a man learneth of himself, and bringeth his own thoughts to light, and whetteth his wits as against a stone, which itself cuts not. In a word, a man were better relate himself to a statue, or picture, then to suffer his thoughts to pass in smother.

Add now, to make this second fruit of friendship complete, that other point, which lieth more open, and falleth within vulgar observation; which is faithful counsel from a friend. Heraclitus saith well, in one of his enigmas; dry light is ever the best. And certain it is, that the light that a man receiveth by counsel from another, is drier, and purer, than that which cometh from his own understanding, and judgement; which is ever infused and drenched in his affections and customs. So as, there is as much difference, between the counsel that a friend giveth and that a man giveth himself, as there is between the counsel of a friend and of a flatterer. For there is no such flatterer as is a man's self; and there is no such remedy, against flattery of a man's self, as the liberty of a friend. Counsel is of two sorts; the one concerning manners, the other concerning business. For the first; the best preservative to keep the mind in health, is the faithful admonition of a friend. The calling of a man's self to a strict account, is a medicine, sometime, too piercing and corrosive. Reading good books of morality is a little flat, and dead. Observing our faults in others is sometimes unproper for our case. But the best receipt (best, I say, to work, and best to take) is the admonition of a friend. It is a strange thing to behold, what gross errors, and extreme absurdities, many (especially of the greater sort) do commit, for want of a friend, to tell them of them; to the great damage, both of their fame, and fortune. For, as St James saith, they are as men, that look sometimes into a glass, and presently forget their own shape, and favour. As for business, a man may think, if he will, that two eyes see no more than one; or that a gamester seeth always more than a looker on; or that a man in anger is as wise as he, that hath said over the four and twenty letters; or that a musket may be shot off, as well upon the arm, as upon a rest; and such other fond and high imaginations, to think himself all in all. But when all is done, the help of good counsel is that which setteth business straight. And if any man think that he will take counsel, but it shall be by pieces; asking counsel in one business of one man, and in another business of another man; it is well (that is to say, better perhaps than if he asked none at all); but he runneth two dangers: one, that he shall not be faithfully counselled; for it is a rare thing, except it be from a perfect and entire friend, to have counsel given, but such as shall be bowed and crooked to some ends, which he hath that giveth it. The other, that he shall have counsel given, hurtful, and unsafe (though with good meaning), and mixed, partly of mischief, and partly of remedy: even as if you would call a physician, that is thought good, for the cure of the disease you complain of, but is unacquainted with your body; and therefore, may put you in way for a present cure, but overthroweth your health in some other kind; and so cure the disease, and kill the patient. But a friend that is wholly acquainted with a man's estate, will beware by furthering any present business, how he dasheth upon other inconvenience. And therefore, rest not upon scattered counsel; they will rather distract, and mislead, than settle, and direct.

After these two noble fruits of frendship (peace in the affections and support of the judgement) followeth the last fruit; which is like the pomegranate full of many kernels; I mean aid and bearing a part in all actions and occasions. Here, the best way to represent to life the manifold use of frendship is to cast and see, how many things there are, which a man cannot do himself; and then it will appear, that it was a sparing speech of the ancients, to say that a friend is another himself: for that a friend is far more than himself. Men have their time, and die many times in desire of some things, which they principally take to heart; the bestowing of a child, the finishing of a work, or the like. If a man have a true friend, he may rest almost secure, that the care of those things will continue after him. So that a man hath as it were two lives in his desires. A man hath a body, and that body is confined to a place; but where friendship is, all offices of life are as it were granted to him, and his deputy. For he may exercise them by his friend. How many things are there, which a man cannot, with any face or comeliness, say or do himself? A man can scarce allege his own merits with modesty, much less extol them: a man cannot sometimes brook to supplicate or beg: and a number of the like. But all these things, are graceful in a friend's mouth, which are blushing in a man's own. So again, a man's person hath many proper relations, which he cannot put off. A man cannot speak to his son, but as a father; to his wife, but as a husband; to his enemy, but upon terms: whereas a friend may speak, as the case requires, and not as it sorteth with the person. But to enumerate these things were endless: I have given the rule, where a man cannot fitly play his own part: if he have not a friend, he may quit the stage.

28

Of Expense

Riches are for spending; and spending for honour and good actions. Therefore extraordinary expense must be limited by the worth of the occasion: for voluntary undoing may be as well for a man's country as for the kingdom of heaven. But ordinary expense ought to be limited by a man's estate; and governed with such regard, as it be within his compass; and not subject to deceit and abuse of servants; and ordered to the best show, that the bills may be less than the estimation abroad. Certainly, if a man will keep but of even hand, his ordinary expenses ought to be but to the half of his receipts; and if he think to wax rich, but to the third part. It is no baseness, for the greatest, to descend and look into their own estate. Some forbear it, not upon negligence alone, but doubting to bring themselves into melancholy, in respect they shall find it broken. But wounds cannot be cured without searching. He that cannot look into his own estate at all, had need both choose well, those whom he employeth, and change them often: for new are more timorous, and less subtle. He that can look into his estate but seldom, it behoveth him to turn all to certainties. A man had need, if he be plentiful in some kind of expense, to be as saving again, in some other. As if he be plentiful in diet, to be saving in apparel: if he be plentiful in the hall, to be saving in the stable: and the like. For he that is plentiful in expenses of all kinds, will hardly be preserved from decay. In clearing of a man's estate, he may as well hurt himself in being too sudden, as in letting it run on too long. For hasty selling is commonly as disadvantageable as interest. Besides, he that clears at once, will relapse; for finding himself out of straits, he will revert to his customs: but he that cleareth by degrees, induceth a habit of frugality, and gaineth as well upon his mind, as upon his estate. Certainly, who hath a state to repair, may not despise small things: and commonly, it is less dishonourable to abridge petty charges than to stoop to petty gettings. A man ought warily to begin charges, which once begun will continue: but in matters that return not, he may be more magnificent.

29

Of the True Greatness of Kingdoms & Estates

The speech of Themistocles the Athenian, which was haughty and
arrogant, in taking so much to himself, had been a grave and wise
observation and censure, applied at large to others. Desired at a feast
to touch a lute, he said; He could not fiddle, but yet he could make a
small town, a great city. These words (holpen a little with a
metaphor) may express two differing abilities, in those that deal in
business of estate. For if a true survey be taken, of counsellors and
statesmen, there may be found (though rarely) those which can make
a small state great and yet cannot fiddle: as on the other side, there
will be found a great many, that can fiddle very cunningly, but yet are
so far from being able to make a small state great as their gift lieth the
other way; to bring a great and flourishing estate to ruin and decay.
And certainly, those degenerate arts and shifts, whereby many
counsellor and governors gain both favour with their masters, and
estimation with the vulgar, deserve no better name then fiddling;
being things rather pleasing for the time, and graceful to themselves
only, than tending to the weal and advancement of the state which
they serve. There are also (no doubt) counsellor and governors,
which may be held sufficient (*negotiis pares*), able to manage affairs,
and to keep them from precipices and manifest inconveniences;
which nevertheless, are far from the ability to raise and amplify an
estate, in power, means, and fortune. But be the workmen what they
may be, let us speak of the work; that is, the true greatness of
kingdoms and estates; and the means thereof. An argument, fit for
great and mighty princes to have in their hand; to the end, that
neither by over-measuring their forces, they lose themselves in vain

enterprises; nor on the other side, by undervaluing them, they descend to fearful and pusillanimous counsels.

The greatness of an estate in bulk and territory doth fall under measure; and the greatness of finances and revenue doth fall under computation. The population may appear by musters: and the number and greatness of cities and towns, by cards and maps. But yet there is not anything amongst civil affairs more subject to error, than the right valuation, and true judgement, concerning the power and forces of an estate. The kingdom of Heaven is compared, not to any great kernel or nut, but to a grain of mustard-seed; which is one of the least grains, but hath in it a property and spirit, hastily to get up and spread. So are there states, great in territory, and yet not apt to enlarge, or command; and some, that have but a small dimension of stem, and yet apt to be the foundations of great monarchies.

Walled towns, stored arsenals and armouries, goodly races of horse, chariots of war, elephants, ordnance, artillery, and the like: all this is but a sheep in a lion's skin, except the breed and disposition of the people be stout and warlike. Nay, number (itself) in armies, importeth not much, where the people is of weak courage: for (as Virgil saith) It never troubles a wolf how many the sheep be. The army of the Persians in the plains of Arbela was such a vast sea of people, as it did somewhat astonish the commanders in Alexander's army; who came to him therefore, and wished him to set upon them by night; but he answered, he would not pilfer the victory. And the defeat was easy. When Tigranes the Armenian, being encamped upon a hill, with four hundred thousand men, discovered the army of the Romans being not above fourteen thousand marching towards him, he made himself merry with it, and said; Yonder men are too many for an ambassage and too few for a fight. But before the sun set, he found them enough to give him the chase, with infinite slaughter. Many are the examples, of the great odds between number and courage: so that a man may truly make a judgement, that the principal point of greatness in any state is to have a race of military men. Neither is money the sinews of war (as it is trivially said), where the sinews of men's arms, in base and effeminate people, are failing. For Solon said well to Croesus (when in ostentation he showed him his gold), Sir, if any other come that hath better iron than you he will be master of all this gold. Therefore let any prince or state think soberly of his forces, except his militia of natives be of good and valiant soldiers. And let princes, on the other side, that have subjects of martial disposition, know their own strength; unless they be otherwise wanting unto themselves. As for mercenary forces (which is the help in this case), all examples show; that, whatsoever estate or prince doth rest upon them, he may spread his feathers for a time but he will mew them soon after.

The blessing of Judah and Issachar will never meet; that the same people or nation, should be both the lion's whelp and the ass between burthens: neither will it be, that a people over-laid with taxes should ever become valiant, and martial. It is true, that taxes levied by consent of the estate, do abate men's courage less; as it hath been seen notably, in the excises of the Low Countries; and in some degree, in the subsidies of England. For you must note, that we speak now of the heart, and not of the purse. So that, although the same tribute and tax laid by consent, or by imposing, be all one to the purse, yet it works diversely upon the courage. So that you may conclude; that no people over-charged with tribute is fit for empire.

Let states that aim at greatness, take heed how their nobility and gentlemen do multiply too fast. For that maketh the common subject grow to be a peasant, and base swain, driven out of heart, and in effect but the gentleman's labourer. Even as you may see in coppice woods; if you leave your staddles too thick, you shall never have clean underwood, but shrubs and bushes. So in countries, if the gentlemen be too many, the commons will be base; and you will bring it to that, that not the hundred poll will be fit for an helmet: especially as to the infantry, which is the nerve of an army: and so there will be great population, and little strength. This, which I speak of, hath been nowhere better seen, then by comparing of England and France; whereof England, though far less in territory and population, hath been (nevertheless) an overmatch; in regard, the middle people of England make good soldiers, which the peasants of France do not. And herein, the device of King Henry the Seventh, (whereof I have spoken largely in the history of his life) was profound, and admirable; in making farms, and houses of husbandry, of a standard; that is, maintained with such a proportion of land unto them, as may breed a subject to live in convenient plenty, and no servile condition; and to keep the plough in the hands of the owners, and not mere hirelings. And thus indeed, you shall attain to Virgil's character, which he gives to ancient Italy:

terra potens armis atque ubere glebae.

Neither is that state (which for anything I know, is almost peculiar to England and hardly to be found anywhere else, except it be perhaps in Poland) to be passed over; I mean the state of free servants and attendants upon noblemen and gentlemen; which are no ways inferior unto the yeomanry for arms. And therefore, out of all question, the splendour, and magnificence, and great retinues, and hospitality of noblemen and gentlemen received into custom, doth much conduce unto martial greatness. Whereas, contrariwise, the close and reserved living of noblemen and gentlemen causeth a penury of military forces.

By all means, it is to be procured, that the trunk of Nebuchadnezzar's tree of monarchy be great enough to bear the branches, and the boughs; that is, that the natural subjects of the crown or state bear a sufficient proportion to the stronger subjects that they govern. Therefore all states, that are liberal of naturalisation towards strangers, are fit for empire. For to think that an handful of people can, with the greatest courage and policy in the world, embrace too large extent of dominion, it may hold for a time, but it will fail suddenly. The Spartans were a nice people, in point of naturalisation; whereby, while they kept their compass, they stood firm; but when they did spread, and their boughs were becoming too great for their stem, they became a windfall upon the sudden. Never any state was, in this point, so open to receive strangers into their body, as were the Romans. Therefore it sorted with them accordingly; for they grew to the greatest monarchy. Their manner was, to grant naturalisation (which they called *ius civitatis*), and to grant it in the highest degree; that is, not only *ius commercii, ius connubii, ius hereditatis*; but also, *ius suffragii*, and *ius honorum*. And this, not to singular persons alone, but likewise to whole families; yea to cities, and sometimes to nations. Add to this, their custom of plantation of colonies; whereby the Roman plant was removed into the soil of other nations. And putting both constitutions together, you will say, that it was not the Roman that spread upon the world; but it was the world that spread upon the Romans: and that was the sure way of greatness. I have marvelled sometimes at Spain, how they clasp and contain so large dominions, with so few natural Spaniards: but sure, the whole compass of Spain is a very great body of a tree; far above Rome and Sparta at the first. And besides, though they have not had that usage, to naturalise liberally; yet they have that, which is next to it; that is, to employ almost indifferently all nations in their militia of ordinary soldiers: yea, and sometimes in their highest commands. Nay, it seemeth at this instant, they are sensible of this want of natives; as by the Pragmatical Sanction, now published, appeareth.

It is certain, that sedentary and within-door arts, and delicate manufactures (that require rather the finger than the arm) have, in their nature, a contrariety to a military disposition. And generally, all warlike people are a little idle; and love danger better then travail: neither must they be too much broken of it, if they shall be preserved in vigour. Therefore, it was great advantage, in the ancient states of Sparta, Athens, Rome and others, that they had the use of slaves which commonly did rid those manufactures. But that is abolished, in greatest part, by the Christian law. That which cometh nearest to it, is to leave those arts chiefly to strangers (which for that purpose are the more easily to be received), and to contain the principal bulk of the vulgar natives, within those three kinds; tillers of the ground; free servants; and handy-craftsmen of strong and manly arts, as smiths, masons, carpenters, etc.; not reckoning professed soldiers.

But above all, for empire and greatness, it importeth most; that a nation do profess arms, as their principal honour, study, and occupation. For the things, which we formerly have spoken of, are but habitations towards arms: and what is habilitation without intention and act? Romulus, after his death (as they report, or feign) sent a present to the Romans; that, above all, they should intend arms; and then, they should prove the greatest empire of the world. The fabric of the state of Sparta was wholly (though not wisely) framed, and composed, to that scope and end. The Persians and Macedonians had it for a flash. The Gauls, Germans, Goths, Saxons, Normans and others, had it for a time. The Turks have it, at this day, though in great declination. Of Christian Europe, they that have it, are, in effect, only the Spaniards. But it is so plain, that every man profiteth in that he most intendeth, that it needeth not to be stood upon. It is enough to point at it; that no nation, which doth not directly profess arms, may look to have greatness fall into their mouths. And, on the other side, it is a most certain oracle of time; that those states, that continue long in that profession (as the Romans and Turks principally have done) do wonders. And those that have professed arms but for an age, have notwithstanding commonly attained that greatness in that age, which maintained them long after, when their profession and exercise of arms hath grown to decay.

Incident to this point is; for a state, to have those laws or customs, which may reach forth unto them just occasions (as may be pretended) of war. For there is that justice imprinted in the nature of men, that they enter not upon wars (whereof so many calamities do ensue) but upon some, at the least specious, grounds and quarrels. The Turk hath at hand, for cause of war, the propagation of his law or sect; a quarrel that he may always command. The Romans, though they esteemed the extending the limits of their empire to be great honour to their generals, when it was done, yet they never rested upon that alone, to begin a war. First therefore, let nations, that pretend to greatness, have this; that they be sensible of wrongs, either upon borderers, merchants, or politic ministers; and that they sit not too long upon a provocation. Secondly, let them be pressed and ready to give aids and succours, to their confederates: as it ever was with the Roman: in so much, as if the confederate had leagues defensive with divers other states, and upon invasion offered, did implore their aids severally, yet the Romans would ever be the foremost, and leave it to none other to have the honour. As for the wars which were anciently made on the behalf of a kind of party, or tacit conformity of estate, I do not see how they may be well justified: as when the Romans made a war for the liberty of Greece: or when the Lacedaemonians and Athenians made wars, to set up or pull down democracies, and oligarchies: or when wars were made by foreigners, under the pretence of justice, or protection, to deliver the subjects of others from tyranny, and oppression; and the like. Let it suffice, that no estate expect to be great that is not awake, upon any just occasion of arming.

No body can be healthful without exercise, neither natural body, nor politic: and certainly, to a kingdom or estate, a just and honourable war is the true exercise. A civil war, indeed, is like the heat of a fever; but a foreign war is like the heat of exercise, and serveth to keep the body in health: for in a slothful peace, both courages will effeminate, and manners corrupt. But howsoever it be for happiness, without all question, for greatness it maketh to be still, for the most part, in arms: and the strength of a veteran army (though it be a chargeable business), always on foot, is that, which commonly giveth the law, or at least the reputation amongst all neighbour states;

as may well be seen in Spain; which hath had, in one part or other, a veteran army, almost continually, now by the space of six-score years.

To be master of the sea is an abridgement of a monarchy. Cicero writing to Atticus, of Pompey his preparation against Caesar, saith; *consilium Pompeii plane Themistocleum est; putat enim, qui mari potitur, eumrerumpotiri.* And, without doubt, Pompey had tired out Caesar, if upon vain confidence, he had not left that way. We see the great effects of battles by sea. The battle of Actium decided the empire of the world. The battle of Lepanto arrested the greatness of the Turks. There be many examples, where sea-fights have been final to the war; but this is, when princes or states have set up their rest upon the battles. But thus much is certain; that he that commands the sea is at great liberty, and may take as much, and as little of the war, as he will. Whereas those that be strongest by land, are many times nevertheless in great straits. Surely, at this day, with us of Europe, the vantage of strength at sea (which is one of the principal dowries of this kingdom of Great Britain) is great: both because, most of the kingdoms of Europe are not merely inland, but girt with the sea, most part of their compass; and because, the wealth of both Indies seems in great part but an accessory to the command of the seas.

The wars of latter ages seem to be made in the dark, in respect of the glory and honour, which reflected upon men, from the wars in ancient time. There be now, for martial encouragement, some degrees and orders of chivalry; which nevertheless, are conferred promiscuously upon soldiers and no soldiers; and some remembrance perhaps upon the scutcheon; and some hospitals for maimed soldiers; and such like things. But in ancient times; the trophies erected upon the place of the victory; the funeral laudatives and monuments for those that died in the wars; the crowns and garlands personal; the style of emperor, which the great kings of the world after borrowed; the triumphs of the generals upon their return; the great donatives and largesses upon the disbanding of the armies; were things able to inflame all men's courage. But above all, that of the triumph, amongst the Romans, was not pageants or gaudery, but one of the wisest and noblest institutions that ever was. For it contained three things; honour to the general; riches to the treasury out of the spoils; and donatives to the army. But that honour, perhaps, were not fit for monarchies; except it be in the person of the monarch himself, or his sons; as it came to pass, in the times of the Roman emperors, who did appropriate the actual triumphs to themselves, and their sons, for such wars as they did achieve in person: and left only, for wars achieved by subjects, some triumphal garments, and ensigns, to the general.

To conclude; no man can, by care taking (as the scripture saith) add a cubit to his stature, in this little model of man's body: but in the great frame of kingdoms, and commonwealths, it is in the power of princes, or estates, to add amplitude and greatness to their kingdoms. For by introducing such ordinances, constitutions, and customs, as we have now touched, they may sow greatness to their posterity, and succession. But these things are commonly not observed, but left to take their chance.

30

Of Regiment of Health

There is a wisdom in this, beyond the rules of physic: a man's own observation, what he finds good of, and what he finds hurt of, is the best physic to preserve health. But it is a safer conclusion to say; this agreeth not well with me, therefore I will not continue it; than this; I find no offence of this, therefore I may use it. For strength of nature in youth passeth over many excesses, which are owing a man till his age. Discern of the coming on of years, and think not, to do the same things still; for age will not be defied. Beware of sudden change in any great point of diet, and if necessity enforce it, fit the rest to it. For it is a secret, both in nature, and state; that it is safer to change many things, than one. Examine thy customs, of diet, sleep, exercise, apparel, and the like; and try in anything thou shalt judge hurtful, to discontinue it by little and little; but so, as if thou doest find any inconvenience by the change, thou come back to it again: for it is hard to distinguish, that which is generally held good, and whole-some, from that, which is good particularly, and fit for thine own body. To be free minded, and cheerfully disposed, at hours of meat, and of sleep, and of exercise, is one of the best precepts of long lasting. As for the passions and studies of the mind; avoid envy; anxious fears; anger fretting inwards; subtle and knotty inquisitions; joys, and exhilarations in excess; sadness not communicated. Enter-tain hopes; mirth rather than joy; variety of delights, rather than surfeit of them; wonder, and admiration, and therefore novelties; studies that fill the mind with splendid and illustrious objects, as histories, fables, and contemplations of nature. If you fly physic in health altogether, it will be too strange for your body, when you shall need it. If you make it too familiar, it will work no extraordinary effect, when sickness cometh. I commend rather some diet, for certain seasons, than frequent use of physic, except it be grown into a custom. For those diets alter the body more, and trouble it less. Despise no new accident in your body, but ask opinion of it. In sickness, respect health principally; and in health, action. For those that put their bodies to endure in health, may in most sickness, which are not very sharp, be cured only with diet, and tendering. Celsus could never have spoken it as a physician, had he not been a wise man withal, when he giveth it, for one of the great precepts of health and lasting, that a man do vary, and interchange contraries; but with an inclination to the more benign extreme: use fasting, and full eating, but rather full eating; watching and sleep, but rather sleep; sitting, and exercise, but rather exercise; and the like. So shall nature be cherished, and yet taught masteries. Physicians are some of them so pleasing, and conformable to the humour of the patient, as they press not the true cure of the disease; and some other are so regular, in proceeding according to art, for the disease, as they respect not sufficiently the condition of the patient. Take one of a middle temper; or if it may not be found in one man, combine two of either sort: and forget not to call, as well the best acquainted with your body, as the best reputed of for his faculty.

31

Of Suspicion

Suspicions amongst thoughts, are like bats amongst birds, they ever fly by twilight. Certainly, they are to be repressed, or, at the least, well guarded: for they cloud the mind; they lose friends; and they check with business, whereby business cannot go on currently, and constantly. They dispose kings to tyranny, husbands to jealousy, wise men to irresolution and melancholy. They are defects, not in the heart, but in the brain; for they take place in the stoutest natures: as in the example of Henry the Seventh of England: there was not a more suspicious man, nor a more stout. And in such a composition, they do small hurt. For commonly they are not admitted, but with examination, whether they be likely or no? But in fearful natures, they gain ground too fast. There is nothing makes a man suspect much, more than to know little: and therefore men should remedy suspicion, by procuring to know more, and not to keep their suspicions in smother. What would men have? Do they think, those they employ and deal with are saints? Do they not think, they will have their own ends, and be truer to themselves than to them? Therefore, there is no better way to moderate suspicions, than to account upon such suspicions as true, and yet to bridle them as false. For so far a man ought to make use of suspicions, as to provide, as if that should be true that he suspects, yet it may do him no hurt. Suspicions, that the mind of itself gathers, are but buzzes; but suspicions, that are artificially nourished, and put into men's heads, by the tales, and whisperings of others, have stings. Certainly, the best mean to clear the way in this same wood of suspicions, is frankly to communicate them with the party that he suspects: for thereby, he shall be sure to know more of the truth of them, than he did before; and withal, shall make that party more circumspect, not to give further cause of suspicion. But this would not be done to men of base natures: for they, if they find themselves once suspected, will never be true. The Italian says: *sospetto licentia fede*: as if suspicion did give a passport to faith: but it ought rather to kindle it, to discharge itself.

32

Of Discourse

Some in their discourse, desire rather commendation of wit, in being able to hold all arguments, than of judgment, in discerning what is true: as if it were a praise, to know what might be said, and not what should be thought. Some have certain common places, and themes, wherein they are good, and want variety: which kind of poverty is for the most part tedious, and when it is once perceived ridiculous. The honourablest part of talk is to give the occasion; and again to moderate and pass to somewhat else; for then a man leads the dance. It is good in discourse and speech of conversation, to vary, and intermingle speech of the present occasion with arguments; tales with reasons; asking of questions, with telling of opinions; and jest with earnest: for it is a dull thing to tire, and, as we say now, to jade, anything too far. As for jest, there be certain things, which ought to be privileged from it; namely religion, matters of state, great persons, any man's present business of importance, and any case that deserveth pity. Yet there be some, that think their wits have been asleep, except they dart out somewhat that is piquant, and to the quick: that is a vein which would be bridled;

parce, puer, stimulis, et fortius utere loris.

And generally, men ought to find the difference, between saltness and bitterness. Certainly, he that hath a satyrical vein, as he maketh others afraid of his wit, so he had need be afraid of others' memory. He that questioneth much, shall learn much, and content much; but especially, if he apply his questions to the skill of the persons whom he asketh: for he shall give them occasion, to please themselves in speaking, and himself shall continually gather knowledge. But let his questions not be troublesome; for that is fit for a poser. And let him be sure, to leave other men their turns to speak. Nay, if there be any, that would reign, and take up all the time, let him find means to take them off, and to bring others on; as musicians use to do, with those that dance too long galliards. If you dissemble sometimes your knowledge, of that you are thought to know; you shall be thought another time, to know that, you know not. Speech of a man's self ought to be seldom, and well chosen. I knew one, was wont to say, in scorn; He must needs be a wise man, he speaks so much of himself: and there is but one case, wherein a man may commend himself, with good grace; and that is in commending virtue in another; especially, if it be such a virtue, whereunto himself pretendeth. Speech of touch towards others should be sparingly used: for discourse ought to be as a field, without coming home to any man. I knew two noblemen, of the west part of England; whereof the one was given to scoff, but kept ever royal cheer in his house: the other would ask of those, that had been at the other's table; Tell truly, was there never a flout or dry blow given; to which the guest would answer; Such and such a thing passed: the lord would say; I thought he would mar a good dinner. Discretion of speech is more than eloquence; and to speak agreeably to him, with whom we deal, is more than to speak in good words, or in good order. A good continued speech, without a good speech of interlocution, shows slowness: and a good reply, or second speech, without a good settled speech, showeth shallowness and weakness. As we see in beasts, that those that are weakest in the course, are yet nimblest in the turn: as it is betwixt the greyhound and the hare. To use too many circumstances, ere one come to the matter, is wearisome; to use none at all, is blunt.

33

Of Plantations

Plantations are amongst ancient, primitive, and heroical works. When the world was young, it begat more children; but now it is old, it begets fewer: for I may justly account new plantations, to be the children of former kingdoms. I like a plantation in a pure soil; that is, where people are not displanted, to the end to plant in others. For else, it is rather an extirpation, then a plantation. Planting of countries, is like planting of woods; for you must make account, to lose almost twenty years' profit, and expect your recompense in the end. For the principal thing, that hath been the destruction of most plantations, hath been the base and hasty drawing of profit, in the first years. It is true, speedy profit is not to be neglected, as far as may stand with the good of the plantation, but no further. It is a shameful and unblessed thing, to take the scum of people, and wicked condemned men, to be the people with whom you plant: and not only so, but it spoileth the plantation; for they will ever live like rogues, and not fall to work, but be lazy, and do mischief, and spend victuals, and be quickly weary, and then certify over to their country, to the discredit of the plantation. The people wherewith you plant, ought to be gardeners, ploughmen, labourers, smiths, carpenters, joiners, fishermen, fowlers, with some few apothecaries, surgeons, cooks, and bakers. In a country of plantation, first look about, what kind of victual the country yields of itself, to hand: as chestnuts, walnuts, pineapples, olives, dates, plums, cherries, wild honey, and the like: and make use of them. Then consider, what victual or esculent things there are, which grow speedily, and within the year; as parsnips, carrots, turnips, onions, radish, artichokes of Jerusalem, maize and the like. For wheat, barley and oats, they ask too much labour: but with peas and beans, you may begin; both because they ask less labour, and because they serve for meat, as well as for bread. And of rice likewise cometh a great increase, and it is a kind of meat. Above all, there ought to be brought store of biscuit, oat-meal, flower, meal, and the like, in the beginning, till bread may be had. For beasts, or birds, take chiefly such as are least subject to diseases, and multiply fastest: as swine, goats, cocks, hens, turkeys, geese, house-doves, and the like. The victual in plantations ought to be expended, almost as in a besieged town; that is, with certain allowance. And let the main part of the ground employed to gardens or corn, be to a common stock; and to be laid in, and stored up, and then delivered out in proportion; besides some spots of ground, that any particular person will manure, for his own private. Consider likewise, what commodities the soil, where the plantation is, doth naturally yield, that they may some way help to defray the charge of the plantation: so it be not, as was said, to the untimely prejudice of the main business; as it hath fared with tobacco in Virginia. Wood commonly aboundeth but too much; and therefore, timber is fit to be one. If there be iron ore, and streams whereupon to set the mills; iron is a brave commodity, where wood aboundeth. Making a bay salt, if the climate be proper for it, would be put in experience. Growing silk likewise, if any be, is a likely commodity. Pitch and tar, where store of firs and pines are, will not fail. So drugs, and sweet woods, where they are, cannot but yield great profit. Soap ashes likewise, and other things that may be thought of. But moil not too much under ground: for the hope of mines is very uncertain, and useth to make the planters lazy in other things. For government, let it be in the hands of one, assisted with some counsel: and let them have commission to exercise martial laws, with some limitation. And above all, let men make that profit of being in the wilderness, as they have God always, and his service before their eyes. Let not the government of the plantation depend upon too many counsellors, and undertakers, in the country that planteth, but upon a temperate number; and let those be rather noblemen, and gentlemen, than merchants: for they look ever to the present gain. Let there be freedoms from custom, till the plantation be of strength: and not only freedom from custom, but freedom to carry their commodities, where they may make their best of them, except there be some special cause of caution. Cram not in people, by sending too fast company after company; but rather hearken how they waste, and send supplies proportionably; but so, as the number may live well in the plantation, and not by surcharge be in penury. It hath been a great endangering to the health of some plantations, that they have built along the sea, and rivers, in marsh and unwholesome grounds. Therefore, though you begin there, to avoid carriage, and other like discommodities, yet build still rather upwards, from the streams, than along. It concerneth likewise the health of the plantation, that they have good store of salt with them, that they may use it in their victuals, when it shall be necessary. If you plant, where savages are, do not only entertain them with trifles, and gingles; but use them justly, and graciously, with sufficient guard nevertheless: and do not win their favour, by helping them to invade their enemies, but for their defence it is not amiss: and send oft of them, over to the country that plants, that they may see a better condition then their own, and commend it when they return. When the plantation grows to strength, then it is time to plant with women, as well as with men; that the plantation may spread into generations, and not be ever pieced from without. It is the sinfullest thing in the world, to forsake or destitute a plantation, once in forwardness: for besides the dishonour, it is the guiltiness of blood of many commiserable persons.

34

Of Riches

I cannot call riches better than the baggage of virtue. The Roman word is better, *impedimenta*. For as the baggage is to an army, so is riches to virtue. It cannot be spared, nor left behind, but it hindreth the march; yea, and the care of it, sometimes, loseth or disturbeth the victory: of great riches, there is no real use, except it be in the distribution; the rest is but conceit. So saith Solomon; Where much is, there are many to consume it; and what hath the owner, but the sight of it with his eyes? The personal fruition in any man, cannot reach to feel great riches: there is a custody of them; or a power of dole and donative of them; or a fame of them; but no solid use to the owner. Do you not see, what feigned prices are set upon little stones, and rarities? And what works of ostentation are undertaken, because there might seem to be some use of great riches? But then you will say, they may be of use, to buy men out of dangers or troubles. As Solomon saith; Riches are as a strong hold, in the imagination of the rich man. But this is excellently expressed, that it is in imagination, and not always in fact. For certainly great riches have sold more men, than they have bought out. Seek not proud riches, but such as thou mayest get justly, use soberly, distribute cheerfully, and leave content-edly. Yet have no abstract nor friarly contempt of them. But distinguish, as Cicero saith well of Rabirius Postumus; *in studio rei amplificandae apparebat non avaritiae praedam, sed instrumentum bonitati, quaeri.* Hearken also to Solomon, and beware of hasty gathering of riches: *qui festinat ad divitias, non erit insons.* The poets feign that when Plutus (which is riches) is sent from Jupiter, he limps, and goes slowly; but when he is sent from Pluto, he runs, and is swift of foot. Meaning, that riches gotten by good means, and just labour, pace slowly; but when they come by the death of others (as by the course

of inheritance, testaments, and the like), they come tumbling upon a
man. But it mought be applied likewise to Pluto, taking him for the
devil. For when riches come from the devil (as by fraud, and
oppression, and unjust means), they come upon speed. The ways to
enrich are many, and most of them foul. Parsimony is one of the best,
and yet is not innocent: for it withholdeth men from works of
liberality, and charity. The improvement of the ground, is the most
natural obtaining of riches; for it is our great mother's blessing, the
earth's; but it is slow. And yet, where men of great wealth do stoop to
husbandry, it multiplieth riches exceedingly. I knew a nobleman in
England, that had the greatest audits of any man in my time: a great
grazier, a great sheep-master, a great timber man, a great collier, a
great corn-master, a great lead-man, and so of iron, and a number of
the like points of husbandry. So as the earth seemed a sea to him, in
respect of the perpetual importation. It was truly observed by one,
that himself came very hardly to a little riches, and very easily to great
riches. For when a man's stock is come to that, that he can expect the
prime of markets, and overcome those bargains, which for their
greatness are few men's money, and be partner in the industries of
younger men, he cannot but increase mainly. The gains of ordinary
trades and vocations are honest; and furthered by two things, chiefly:
by diligence; and by a good name, for good and fair dealing. But the
gains of bargains are of a more doubtful nature; when men shall wait
upon others' necessity, broke by servants and instruments to draw
them on, put off others cunningly that would be better chapmen, and
the like practices, which are crafty and naught. As for the chopping of
bargains, when a man buys not to hold, but to sell over again, that
commonly grindeth double, both upon the seller and upon the
buyer. Sharings do greatly enrich, if the hands be well chosen, that are
trusted. Usury is the certainest means of gain, though one of the
worst; as that, whereby a man doth eat his bread; *in sudore vultus alieni*:
and besides, doth plough upon Sundays. But yet, certain though it be,
it hath flaws; for that the scriveners and brokers do value unsound
men, to serve their own turn. The fortune, in being the first in an
invention, or in a privilege, doth cause sometimes a wonderful
overgrowth in riches; as it was with the first sugar man, in the
Canaries: therefore, if a man can play the true logician, to have as well
judgement as invention, he may do great matters; especially if the
times be fit. He that resteth upon gains certain, shall hardly grow to

great riches: and he that puts all upon adventures, doth often times break, and come to poverty: it is good therefore, to guard adventures with certainties, that may uphold losses. Monopolies, and coemption of wares for resale, where they are not restrained, are great means to enrich; especially if the party have intelligence what things are like to come into request, and so store himself beforehand. Riches gotten by service, though it be of the best rise, yet when they are gotten by flattery, feeding humours, and other servile conditions, they may be placed amongst the worst. As for fishing for testaments and executorships (as Tacitus saith of Seneca; *testamenta et orbos, tanquam indagine capi*) it is yet worse; by how much men submit themselves to meaner persons than in service. Believe not much them, that seem to despise riches: for they despise them, that despair of them; and none worse, when they come to them. Be not penny-wise; riches have wings, and sometimes they fly away of themselves, sometimes they must be set flying to bring in more. Men leave their riches, either to their kindred; or to the public: and moderate portions prosper best in both. A great state left to an heir, is as a lure to all the birds of prey round about, to seize on him, if he be not the better established in years and judgement. Likewise glorious gifts and foundations are like sacrifices without salt; and but the painted sepulchres of alms, which soon will putrefy, and corrupt inwardly. Therefore, measure not thine advancements by quantity, but frame them by measure; and defer not charities till death: for certainly, if a man weigh it rightly, he that doth so, is rather liberal of another man's, than of his own.

35

Of Prophecies

I mean not to speak of divine prophecies; nor of heathen oracles; nor of natural predictions; but only of prophecies, that have been of certain memory, and from hidden causes. Saith the Pythonissa to Saul; Tomorrow thou and thy son shall be with me. Homer hath these verses:

> at domus Aeneae cunctis dominabitur oris,
> et nati natorum, et qui nascentur ab illis:

a prophecy, as it seems, of the Roman Empire. Seneca the tragedian hath these verses:

> venient annis
> secula seris, quibus Oceanus
> vincula rerum laxet, et ingens
> pateat tellus, Tiphysque novos
> detegat orbes; nec sit terris
> ultima Thule:

a prophecy of the discovery of America. The daughter of Polycrates dreamed that Jupiter bathed her father, and Apollo anointed him: and it came to pass, that he was crucified in an open place, where the sun made his body run with sweat, and the rain washed it. Philip of Macedon dreamed, he sealed up his wife's belly: whereby he did expound it, that his wife should be barren: but Aristander the soothsayer told him, his wife was with child, because men do not use to seal vessels that are empty. A phantasm that appeared to M. Brutus in his tent said to him; *Philippis iterum me videbis.* Tiberius said to Galba: *tu quoque, Galba, degustabis imperium.* In Vespasian's time, there went a prophecy in the East; that those that should come forth of

Judea, should reign over the world: which though it may be was meant of our saviour, yet Tacitus expounds it of Vespasian. Domitian dreamed, the night before he was slain, that a golden head was growing out of the nape of his neck: and indeed, the succession that followed him, for many years, made golden times. Henry the Sixth of England, said of Henry the Seventh, when he was a lad, and gave him water; This is the lad, that shall enjoy the crown, for which we strive. When I was in France, I heard from one Dr Pena, that the Queen Mother, who was given to curious arts, caused the King her husband's nativity to be calculated under a false name; and the astrologer gave a judgement, that he should be killed in a duel; at which the Queen laughed, thinking her husband to be above challenges and duels: but he was slain, upon a course at tilt, the splinters of the staff of Mongomery going in at his beaver. The trivial prophecy, which I heard, when I was a child, and Queen Elizabeth was in the flower of her years, was;

> When hempe is spun,
> England's done.

Whereby, it was generally conceived, that after the princes had reigned, which had the principal letters of that word hempe (which were Henry, Edward, Mary, Philip, and Elizabeth), England should come to utter confusion: which, thanks be to God, is verified only in the change of the name: for that the King's style is now no more of England, but of Britain. There was also another prophecy, before the year of 1688, which I do not well understand:

> There shall be seen upon a day,
> Between the baugh, and the may,
> The black fleet of Norway.
> When that that is come and gone,
> England build houses of lime and stone
> For after wars shall you have none.

It was generally conceived, to be meant of the Spanish fleet, that came in 1688. For that the King of Spain's surname, as they say, is Norway. The prediction of Regiomontanus;

> *octogesimus octavus mirabilis annus*;

was thought likewise accomplished, in the sending of that great fleet, being the greatest in strength, though not in number, of all that ever swam upon the sea. As for Cleon's dream, I think it was a jest. It was, that he was devoured of a long dragon; and it was expounded of a maker of sausages, that troubled him exceedingly. There are numbers of the like kind; especially if you include dreams, and predictions of astrology. But I have set down these few only of certain credit, for example. My judgement is, that they ought all to be despised; and ought to serve, but for winter talk by the fireside. Though when I say despised, I mean it as for belief: for otherwise, the spreading or publishing of them is in no sort to be despised. For they have done much mischief: and I see many severe laws made to suppress them. That, that hath given them grace, and some credit, consisteth in three things. First, that men mark, when they hit, and never mark, when they miss: as they do, generally, also of dreams. The second is, that probable conjectures, or obscure traditions, many times turn themselves into prophecies: while the nature of man, which coveteth divination, thinks it no peril to foretell that, which indeed they do but collect. As that of Seneca's verse. For so much was then subject to demonstration, that the globe of the earth had great parts beyond the Atlantic; which mought be probably conceived, not to be all sea: and adding thereto the tradition in Plato's *Timáeus*, and his *Atlanticus*, it mought encourage one, to turn it to a prediction. The third, and last (which is the great one) is, that almost all of them, being infinite in number, have been impostures, and by idle and crafty brains, merely contrived and feigned, after the event past.

36

Of Ambition

Ambition is like choler; which is an humour, that maketh men active, earnest, full of alacrity, and stirring, if it be not stopped. But if it be stopped, and cannot have his way, it becometh adust, and thereby malign and venomous. So ambitious men, if they find the way open for their rising, and still get forward, they are rather busy than dangerous; but if they be checked in their desires, they become secretly discontent, and look upon men and matters, with an evil eye; and are best pleased, when things go backward; which is the worst property, in a servant of a prince or state. Therefore it is good for princes, if they use ambitious men, to handle it so, as they be still progressive, and not retrograde: which because it cannot be without inconvenience, it is good not to use such natures at all. For if they rise not with their service, they will take order to make their service fall with them. But since we have said, it were good not to use men of ambitious natures, except it be upon necessity, it is fit we speak in what cases they are of necessity. Good commanders in the wars must be taken, be they never so ambitious: for the use of their service dispenseth with the rest; and to take a soldier without ambition, is to pull off his spurs. There is also great use of ambitious men, in being screens to princes, in matters of danger and envy: for no man will take that part, except he be like a seeled dove, that mounts and mounts, because he cannot see about him. There is use also of ambitious men, in pulling down the greatness of any subject that overtops: as Tiberius used Macro in the pulling down of Seianus. Since therefore they must be used, in such cases, there resteth to speak how they are to be bridled, that they may be less dangerous. There is less danger of them, if they be of mean birth, than if they be noble: and if they be rather harsh of nature, than gracious and popular: and if they be rather new raised, than grown cunning, and fortified in their greatness. It is counted by some a weakness in princes, to have favourites: but it is, of all others, the best remedy against ambitious great-ones. For when the way of pleasuring and displeasuring lieth by the favourite, it is impossible any other should be over-great. Another means to curb them, is to balance them by others as proud as they. But then, there must be some middle counsellors, to keep things steady: for without that ballast, the ship will roll too much. At the least, a prince may animate and inure some meaner persons, to be, as it were, scourges to ambitious men. As for the having of them obnoxious to ruin, if they be of fearful natures, it may do well: but if they be stout, and daring, it may precipitate their designs, and prove dangerous. As for the pulling of them down, if the affairs require it, and that it may not be done with safety suddenly, the only way is the interchange continually of favours, and disgraces; whereby they may not know what to expect; and be, as it were, in a wood. Of ambitions, it is less harmful, the ambition to prevail in great things, than that other, to appear in everything; for that breeds confusion, and mars business. But yet, it is less danger to have an ambitious man stirring in business, than great in dependencies. He that seeketh to be eminent amongst able men, hath a great task; but that is ever good for the public. But he that plots to be the only figure amongst ciphers, is the decay of an whole age. Honour hath three things in it: the vantage ground to do good: the approach to kings, and principal persons: and the raising of a man's own fortunes. He that hath the best of these intentions, when he aspireth, is an honest man: and that prince that can discern of these intentions in another that aspireth, is a wise prince. Generally, let princes and states choose such ministers, as are more sensible of duty, than of rising; and such as love business rather upon con-science, than upon bravery: and let them discern a busy nature, from a willing mind.

37

Of Masques & Triumphs

These things are but toys, to come amongst such serious observations. But yet, since princes will have such things, it is better they should be graced with elegancy, than daubed with cost. Dancing to song, is a thing of great state, and pleasure. I understand it, that the song be in choir, placed aloft, and accompanied with some broken music: and the ditty fitted to the device. Acting in song, especially in dialogues, hath an extreme good grace: I say acting, not dancing (for that is a mean and vulgar thing), and the voices of the dialogue would be strong and manly (a bass, and a tenor; no treble) and the ditty high and tragical; not nice or dainty. Several choirs, placed one over against another, and taking the voice by catches, anthem-wise, give great pleasure. Turning dances into figure is a childish curiosity. And generally, let it be noted, that those things which I here set down, are such as do naturally take the sense, and not respect petty wonderments. It is true, the alterations of scenes, so it be quietly, and without noise, are things of great beauty, and pleasure: for they feed and relieve the eye, before it be full of the same object. Let the scenes abound with light, specially coloured and varied: and let the masquers, or any other, that are to come down from the scene, have some motions upon the scene itself, before their coming down: for it draws the eye strangely, and makes it with great pleasure, to desire to see that it cannot perfectly discern. Let the songs be loud, and cheerful, and not chirpings, or pulings. Let the music likewise be sharp, and loud, and well placed. The colours that show best by candlelight are; white, carnation, and a kind of seawater-green; and oes, or spangs, as they are of no great cost, so they are of most glory. As for rich embroidery, it is lost, and not discerned. Let the suits of the masquers be graceful, and such as become the person, when the vizors are off: not after examples of known attires; Turks, soldiers, mariners, and the like. Let antimasques not be long; they have been commonly of fools, satyrs, baboons, wild-men, antics, beasts, sprites, witches, Ethiopes, pigmies, turquets, nymphs, rustics, cupids, statues moving, and the like. As for angels, it is not comical enough, to put them in anti-masques; and any thing that is hideous, as devils, giants, is on the other side as unfit. But chiefly, let the music of them be recreative, and with some strange changes. Some sweet odours, suddenly coming forth, without any drops falling, are, in such a company, as there is steam and heat, things of great pleasure and refreshment. Double masques, one of men, another of ladies, addeth state and variety. But all is nothing, except the room be kept clear and neat.

For justs, and tourneys, and barriers; the glories of them are chiefly in the chariots, wherein the challengers make their entry; especially if they be drawn with strange beasts; as lions, bears, camels, and the like: or in the devices of their entrance; or in the bravery of their liveries; or in the goodly furniture of their horses, and armour. But enough of these toys.

38

Of Nature in Men

Nature is often hidden; sometimes overcome; seldom extinguished.
Force maketh nature more violent in the return: doctrine and
discourse maketh nature less importune: but custom only doth alter
and subdue nature. He that seeketh victory over his nature, let him
not set himself too great, nor too small tasks: for the first will make
him dejected by often failings; and the second will make him a small
proceeder, though by often prevailings. And at the first, let him
practise with helps, as swimmers do with bladders, or rushes: but after
a time, let him practise with disadvantages, as dancers do with thick
shoes. For it breeds great perfection, if the practice be harder then the
use. Where nature is mighty, and therefore the victory hard, the
degrees had need be; first to stay and arrest nature in time; like to
him, that would say over the four and twenty letters, when he was
angry: then to go less in quantity; as if one should, in forbearing wine,
come from drinking healths, to a draught at a meal: and lastly, to
discontinue altogether. But if a man have the fortitude, and resolution,
to enfranchise himself at once, that is the best;

> *optimus ille animi vindex, laedentia pectus*
> *vincula qui rupit, dedoluitque semel.*

Neither is the ancient rule amiss, to bend nature as a wand, to a
contrary extreme, whereby to set it right: understanding it, where the
contrary extreme is no vice. Let not a man force a habit upon himself,
with perpetual continuance, but with some intermission. For both
the pause reinforceth the new onset; and if a man that is not perfect
be ever in practice, he shall as well practise his errors, as his abilities;
and induce one habit of both: and there is no means to help this, but
by seasonable intermissions. But let not a man trust his victory over

his nature too far; for nature will lay buried a great time, and yet revive, upon the occasion or temptation. Like as it was with Aesop's damsel, turned from a cat to a woman; who sat very demurely, at the board's end, till a mouse ran before her. Therefore let a man either avoid the occasion altogether; or put himself often to it, that he may be little moved with it. A man's nature is best perceived in privateness, for there is no affectation; in passion, for that putteth a man out of his precepts; and in a new case or experiment, for there custom leaveth him. They are happy men, whose natures sort with their vocations; otherwise they may say, *multum incola fuit anima mea*, when they converse in those things, they do not affect. In studies, whatsoever a man commandeth upon himself, let him set hours for it: but whatsoever is agreeable to his nature, let him take no care for any set times: for his thoughts will fly to it of themselves; so as the spaces of other business, or studies, will suffice. A man's nature runs either to herbs, or weeds; therefore let him seasonably water the one, and destroy the other.

39

Of Custom & Education

Men's thoughts are much according to their inclination: their discourse and speeches according to their learning, and infused opinions; but their deeds are after as they have been accustomed. And therefore, as Machiavelli well noteth (though in an evil favoured instance) there is no trusting to the force of nature, nor to the bravery of words; except it be corroborate by custom. His instance is, that for the achieving of a desperate conspiracy, a man should not rest upon the fierceness of any man's nature, or his resolute undertakings; but take such an one, as hath had his hands formerly in blood. But Machiavelli knew not of a Friar Clement, nor a Ravillac, nor a Jaureguy, nor a Baltazar Gerard: yet his rule holdeth still, that nature, nor the engagement of words, are not so forcible as custom. Only superstition is now so well advanced, that men of the first blood are as firm as butchers by occupation: and votary resolution is made equipollent to custom, even in matter of blood. In other things, the predominancy of custom is everywhere visible; in so much, as a man would wonder, to hear men profess, protest, engage, give great words, and then do just as they have done before: as if they were dead images, and engines moved only by the wheels of custom. We see also the reign or tyranny of custom, what it is. The Indians (I mean the sect of their wise men) lay themselves quietly upon a stack of wood, and so sacrifice themselves by fire. Nay, the wives strive to be burned with the corpses of their husbands. The lads of Sparta, of ancient time, were wont to be scourged upon the altar of Diana, without so much as queching. I remember in the beginning of Queen Elizabeth's time of England, an Irish rebel condemned, put up a petition to the deputy, that he might be hanged in a with, and not in an halter, because it had been so used, with former rebels. There be monks in Russia, for penance, that will sit a whole night in a vessel of water, till they be engaged with hard ice. Many examples may be put of the force of custom, both upon mind, and body. Therefore, since custom is the principal magistrate of man's life, let men by all means endeavour to obtain good customs. Certainly, custom is most perfect, when it beginneth in young years: this we call education; which is, in effect, but an early custom. So we see, in languages the tongue is more pliant to all expressions and sounds, the joints are more supple to all fears of activity and motions, in youth than afterwards. For it is true, that late learners cannot so well take the ply; except it be in some minds, that have not suffered themselves to fix, but have kept themselves open and prepared to receive continual amendment, which is exceeding rare. But if the force of custom simple and separate, be great: the force of custom copulate, and conjoined and collegiate, is far greater. For there example teacheth; company comforteth; emulation quickeneth; glory raiseth: so as in such places the force of custom is in his exaltation. Certainly, the great multiplication of virtues upon human nature resteth upon societies well ordained, and disciplined. For commonwealths, and good governments, do nourish virtue grown, but do not much mend the seeds. But the misery is, that the most effectual means are now applied to the ends least to be desired.

40

Of Fortune

It cannot be denied, but outward accidents conduce much to fortune, favour, opportunity, death of others, occasion fitting virtue. But chiefly, the mould of a man's fortune is in his own hands. *Faber quisque fortunae suae*; saith the poet. And the most frequent of external causes is, that the folly of one man is the fortune of another. For no man prospers so suddenly, as by others' errors. *Serpens nisi serpentem comederit non fit draco*. Overt and apparent virtues bring forth praise; but there be secret and hidden virtues, that bring forth fortune; certain deliveries of a man's self, which have no name. The Spanish name, *desemboltura*, partly expresseth them: when there be not stonds, nor restiveness in a man's nature; but that the wheels of his mind keep way with the wheels of his fortune. For so Livy (after he had described Cato Major, in these words; *in illo viro, tantum robur corporis et animi fuit, ut quocunque loco natus esset, fortunam sibi facturus videretur*) falleth upon that, that he had *versatile ingenium*. Therefore, if a man look sharply, and attentively, he shall see fortune: for though she be blind, yet she is not invisible. The way of fortune is like the Milken Way in the sky; which is a meeting or knot of a number of small stars; not seen asunder, but giving light together. So are there a number of little, and scarce discerned virtues, or rather faculties and customs, that make men fortunate. The Italians note some of them, such as a man would little think. When they speak of one that cannot do amiss, they will throw in, into his other conditions, that he hath *poco di matto*. And certainly, there be not two more fortunate properties; than to have a little of the fool; and not too much of the honest. Therefore, extreme lovers of their country, or masters, were never fortunate, neither can they be. For when a man placeth his thoughts without himself, he goeth not his own way. An hasty fortune maketh an enterpriser, and remover (the French hath it better; *entrepreneur*, or *remuant*), but the exercised fortune maketh the able man. Fortune is to be honoured, and respected, and it be but for her daughters, Confidence, and Reputation. For those two felicity breedeth: the first within a man's self; the latter, in others towards him. All wise men, to decline the envy of their own virtues, use to ascribe them to providence and fortune; for so they may the better assume them: and besides, it is greatness in a man, to be the care of the higher powers. So Caesar said to the pilot in the tempest, *Caesarem portas, et fortunam eius*. So Sulla chose the name of Felix, and not of Magnus. And it hath been noted, that those that ascribe openly too much to their own wisdom, and policy, end unfortunate. It is written, that Timotheus the Athenian, after he had, in the account he gave to the state of his government, often interlaced this speech, 'and in this fortune had no part', never prospered in anything he undertook afterwards. Certainly, there be, whose fortunes are like Homer's verses, that have a slide, and easiness, more than the verses of other poets: as Plutarch saith of Timoleon's fortune, in respect of that of Agesilaus, or Epaminondas. And that this should be, no doubt it is much in a man's self.

41

Of Usury

Many have made witty invectives against usury. They say, that it is pity, the devil should have God's part, which is the tithe. That the usurer is the greatest Sabbath breaker, because his plough goeth every Sunday. That the userer is the drone, that Virgil speaketh of:

ignavum fucos pecus a praesepibus arcent.

That the usurer breaketh the first law that was made for mankind, after the fall; which was, *in sudore vultus tui comedes panem tuum*; not, in *sudore vultus alieni*. That usurers should have orange-tawny bonnets, because they do Judaise. That it is against nature, for money to beget money; and the like. I say this only, that usury is a *concessum propter duritiem cordis*: for since there must be borrowing and lending, and men are so hard of heart as they will not lend freely, usury must be permitted. Some others have made suspicious and cunning propositions of banks, discovery of men's estates, and other inventions. But few have spoken of usury usefully. It is good to set before us the incommodities, and commodities of usury; that the good may be either weighed out, or culled out; and warily to provide, that while we make forth to that which is better, we meet not with that which is worse.

The discommodities of usury are: first, that it makes fewer merchants. For were it not for this lazy trade of usury, money would not lie still, but would, in great part, be employed upon merchandising; which is the *vena porta* of wealth in a state. The second, that it makes poor merchants. For as a farmer cannot husband his ground so well, if he sit at a great rent; so the merchant cannot drive his trade so well, if he sit at great usury. The third is incident to the other two; and that is, the decay of customs of kings or states, which ebb or flow with merchandising. The fourth, that it bringeth the treasure of a realm or state into a few hands. For the usurer being at certainties, and others at uncertainties, at the end of the game; most of the money will be in the box; and ever a state flourisheth, when wealth is more equally spread. The fifth, that it beats down the price of land: for the employment of money is chiefly, either merchandising, or purchasing; and usury waylays both. The sixth, that it doth dull and damp all industries, improvements, and new inventions, wherein money would be stirring, if it were not for this slug. The last, that it is the cancer and ruin of many men's estates; which in process of time breeds a public poverty.

On the other side, the commodities of usury are. First, that howsoever usury in some respect hindereth merchandising, yet in some other it advanceth it: for it is certain, that the greatest part of trade is driven by young merchants, upon borrowing at interest: so as if the usurer either call in, or keep back his money, there will ensue presently a great stand of trade. The second is, that were it not for this easy borrowing upon interest, men's necessities would draw upon them a most sudden undoing; in that they would be forced to sell their means (be it lands or goods) far under foot; and so, whereas duty doth but gnaw upon them, bad markets would swallow them quite up. As for mortgaging, or pawning, it will little mend the matter; for either men will not take pawns without use; or if they do, they will look precisely for the forfeiture. I remember a cruel moneyed man, in the country, that would say; the devil take this usury, it keeps us from forfeitures of mortgages and bonds. The third and last is; that it is a vanity to conceive that there would be ordinary borrowing without profit; and it is impossible to conceive the number of inconveniencies that will ensue, if borrowing be cramped. Therefore, to speak of the abolishing of usury is idle. All states have ever had it, in one kind or rate, or other. So as that opinion must be sent to Utopia.

To speak now, of the reformation and reiglement of usury; how the discommodities of it may be best avoided, and the commodities retained. It appears by the balance of commodities and discommodities of usury, two things are to be reconciled. The one, that the tooth of usury be grinded, that it bite not too much: the other, that there be left open a means, to invite moneyed men to lend to the merchants, for the continuing and quickening of trade. This cannot be done, except you introduce two several sorts of usury; a less, and a greater. For if you reduce usury to one low rate, it will ease the common borrower, but the merchant will be to seek for money. And it is to be noted that the trade of merchandise, being the most lucrative, may bear usury at a good rate; other contracts not so.

To serve both intentions, the way would be briefly thus. That there be two rates of usury, the one free, and general for all; the other under licence only, to certain persons, and in certain places of merchandising. First therefore, let usury, in general, be reduced to five in the hundred; and let that rate be proclaimed to be free and current; and let the state shut itself out, to take any penalty for the same. This will preserve borrowing from any general stop or dryness. This will ease infinite borrowers in the country. This will, in good part, raise the price of land, because land purchased at sixteen years purchase will yield six in the hundred, and somewhat more, whereas this rate of interest yields but five. This, by like reason, will encourage and edge industrious and profitable improvements; because many will rather venture in that kind, than take five in the hundred, especially having been used to greater profit. Secondly, let there be certain persons licensed to lend, to known merchants, upon usury at a higher rate; and let it be with the cautions following. Let the rate be, even with the merchant himself, somewhat more easy, than that he used formerly to pay: for, by that means, all borrowers shall have some ease by this reformation, be he merchant, or whosoever. Let it be no rank or common stock, but every man be master of his own money: not that I altogether mislike banks, but they will hardly be brooked, in regard of certain suspicions. Let the state be answered, some small matter, for the licence, and the rest left to the lender: for if the abatement be but small, it will no whit discourage the lender. For he, for example, that took before ten or nine in the hundred, will sooner descend to eight in the hundred, than give over his trade of usury, and go from certain gains, to gains of hazard. Let these licenced lenders be in number indefinite, but restrained to certain principal cities and towns of merchandising: for then they will be hardly able to colour other men's monies in the country: so as the licence of nine will not suck away the current rate of five: for no man will send his monies far off, nor put them into unknown hands.

If it be objected that this doth, in a sort, authorise usury, which before was, in some places, but permissive: the answer is; that it is better to mitigate usury by declaration, than to suffer it to rage by connivance.

42

Of Youth & Age

A man that is young in years, may be old in hours, if he have lost no time. But that happeneth rarely. Generally, youth is like the first cogitations, not so wise as the second. For there is a youth in thoughts as well as in ages. And yet the invention of young men is more lively than that of old: and imaginations stream into their minds better, and, as it were, more divinely. Natures that have much heat, and great and violent desires and perturbations, are not ripe for action, till they have passed the meridian of their years: as it was with Julius Caesar, and Septimius Severus. Of the latter of whom, it is said; *iuventutem egit erroribus, imo furoribus, plenam.* And yet he was the ablest emperor, almost, of all the list. But reposed natures may do well in youth. As it is seen in Augustus Caesar, Cosmus Duke of Florence, Gaston de Fois, and others. On the other side, heat and vivacity in age is an excellent composition for business. Young men are fitter to invent, than to judge; fitter for execution, than for counsel; and fitter for new projects, than for settled business. For the experience of age, in things that fall within the compass of it, directeth them; but in new things, abuseth them. The errors of young men are the ruin of business; but the errors of aged men amount but to this; that more might have been done, or sooner. Young men, in the conduct and manage of actions, embrace more than they can hold, stir more than they can quiet; fly to the end, without consideration of the means, and degrees; pursue some few principles, which they have chanced upon absurdly; care not to innovate, which draws unknown inconveniences; use extreme remedies at first; and, that which doubleth all errors, will not acknowledge or retract them; like an unready horse, that will neither stop, nor turn. Men of age object too much, consult too long, adventure too little, repent too soon, and seldom drive business home to the full period; but content themselves with a mediocrity of success. Certainly, it is good to compound employments of both; for that will be good for the present, because the virtues of either age may correct the defects of both: and good for succession, that young men may be learners, while men in age are actors: and lastly, good for extreme accidents, because authority followeth old men, and favour and popularity youth. But for the moral part, perhaps youth will have the pre-eminence, as age hath for the politic. A certain rabbin, upon the text; Your young men that see visions, and your old men that dream dreams; inferreth, that young men are admitted nearer to God than old; because vision is a clearer revelation, than a dream. And certainly, the more a man drinketh of the world, the more it intoxicateth; and age doth profit rather in the powers of understanding, than in the virtues of the will and affections. There be some have an over-early ripeness in their years, which fadeth betimes: these are first, such as have brittle wits, the edge whereof is soon turned; such as was Hermogenes the Rhetorician, whose books are exceeding subtle; who afterwards waxed stupid. A second sort is of those, that have some natural dispositions, which have better grace in youth, than in age: such as is a fluent and luxuriant speech; which becomes youth well, but not age: so Tully saith of Hortentius; *idem manebat, neque idem decebat*. The third is of such as take too high a strain at the first; and are magnanimous, more than tract of years can uphold. As was Scipio Africanus, of whom Livy saith in effect; *ultima primis cedebant*.

43

Of Beauty

Virtue is like a rich stone, best plain set: and surely virtue is best in a body that is comely, though not of delicate features: and that hath rather dignity of presence, than beauty of aspect. Neither is it almost seen, that very beautiful persons are otherwise of great virtue; as if nature were rather busy not to err, than in labour to produce excellency. And therefore, they prove accomplished, but not of great spirit; and study rather behaviour, than virtue; but this holds not always; for Augustus Caesar, Titus Vespasianus, Philip le Belle of France, Edward the Fourth of England, Alcibiades of Athens, Ismael the Sophy of Persia, were all high and great spirits; and yet the most beautiful men of their times. In beauty, that of favour is more than that of colour, and that of decent and gracious motion, more than that of favour. That is the best part of beauty, which a picture cannot express; no, nor the first sight of the life. There is no excellent beauty, that hath not some strangeness in the proportion. A man cannot tell, whether Apelles, or Albert Durer, were the more trifler: whereof the one would make a personage by geometrical proportions: the other, by taking the best parts out of divers faces, to make one excellent. Such personages, I think, would please nobody but the painter that made them. Not but I think a painter may make a better face, than ever was; but he must do it, by a kind of felicity (as a musician that maketh an excellent air in music) and not by rule. A man shall see faces, that if you examine them, part by part, you shall find never a good; and yet all together do well. If it be true, that the principal part of beauty is in decent motion, certainly it is no marvel though persons in years seem many times more amiable; *pulchrorum autumnus pulcher*: for no youth can be comely but by pardon, and considering the youth as to make up the comeliness. Beauty is as summer fruits, which are easy to corrupt, and cannot last: and, for the most part, it makes a dissolute youth, and an age a little out of countenance: but yet certainly again, if it light well, it maketh virtues shine, and vices blush.

44

Of Deformity

Deformed persons are commonly even with nature: for as nature hath done ill by them, so do they by nature: being for the most part, (as the scripture saith) void of natural affection; and so they have their revenge of nature. Certainly there is a consent between the body and the mind; and where nature erreth in the one, she ventureth in the other. *Ubi peccat in uno, periclitatur in altero.* But because there is in man an election touching the frame of his mind, and a necessity in the frame of his body, the stars of natural inclination are sometimes obscured by the sun of discipline, and virtue. Therefore, it is good to consider of deformity, not as a sign, which is more deceivable; but as a cause, which seldom faileth of the effect. Whosoever hath anything fixed in his person, that doth induce contempt, hath also a perpetual spur in himself, to rescue and deliver himself from scorn: therefore all deformed persons are extreme bold. First, as in their own defence, as being exposed to scorn; but in process of time, by a general habit. Also it stirreth in them industry, and especially of this kind, to watch and observe the weakness of others, that they may have somewhat to repay. Again, in their superiors, it quencheth jealousy towards them, as persons that they think they may at pleasure despise: and it layeth their competitors and emulators asleep; as never believing, they should be in possibility of advancement, till they see them in possession. So that, upon the matter, in a great wit, deformity is an advantage to rising. Kings in ancient times (and at this present in some countries) were wont to put great trust in eunuchs; because they that are envious towards all, are more obnoxious and officious towards one. But yet their trust towards them hath rather been as to good spials, and good whisperers; than good magistrates, and officers. And much like is the reason of deformed persons. Still the ground is, they will, if they be of spirit, seek to free themselves from scorn; which must be, either by virtue, or malice: and therefore, let it not be marvelled, if sometimes they prove excellent persons; as was Agesilaus, Zanger the son of Solyman, Aesop, Gasca President of Peru; and Socrates may go likewise amongst them; with others.

45

Of Building

Houses are built to live in, and not to look on: therefore let use be preferred before uniformity; except where both may be had. Leave the goodly fabrics of houses, for beauty only, to the enchanted palaces of the poets: who build them with small cost. He that builds a fair house, upon an ill seat, committeth himself to prison. Neither do I reckon it an ill seat only where the air is unwholesome; but likewise where the air is unequal; as you shall see many fine seats, set upon a knap of ground, environed with higher hills round about it: whereby the heat of the sun is pent in, and the wind gathereth as in troubles; so as you shall have, and that suddenly, as great diversity of heat and cold, as if you dwelt in several places. Neither is it ill air only that maketh an ill seat, but ill ways, ill markets; and, if you will consult with Momus, ill neighbours. I speak not of many more: want of water; want of wood, shade, and shelter; want of fruitfulness, and mixture of grounds of several natures; want of prospect; want of level grounds; want of places, at some near distance, for sports of hunting, hawking, and races; too near the sea, too remote; having the commodity of navigable rivers, or the discommodity of their overflowing; too far off from great cities, which may hinder business; or too near them, which lurcheth all provisions, and maketh every thing dear: where a man hath a great living laid together, and where he is scanted: all which, as it is impossible, perhaps, to find together, so it is good to know them, and think of them, that a man may take as many as he can: and if he have several dwellings, that he sort them so, that what he wanteth in the one, he may find in the other. Lucullus answered Pompey well; who when he saw his stately galleries, and rooms, so large and lightsome, in one of his houses, said; Surely, an excellent place for summer, but how do you in winter?

Lucullus answered; Why, do you not think me as wise as some fowl are, that ever change their abode towards the winter?

To pass from the seat, to the house itself; we will do as Cicero doth, in the orator's art; who writes books *De Oratore*, and a book he entitles *Orator*: whereof the former delivers the precepts of the art; and the latter the perfection. We will therefore describe a princely palace, making a brief model thereof. For it is strange to see, now in Europe, such huge buildings as the Vatican, and Escurial, and some others be, and yet scarce a very fair room in them.

First therefore, I say, you cannot have a perfect palace, except you have two several sides; a side for the banquet, as is spoken of in the Book of Hester; and a side for the household: the one for feasts and triumphs, and the other for dwelling. I understand both these sides to be not only returns, but parts of the front; and to be uniform without, though severally partitioned within; and to be on both sides of a great and stately tower, in the midst of the front; that as it were, joineth them together, on either hand. I would have on the side of the banquet, in front, one only goodly room, above stairs, of some forty foot high; and under it, a room for a dressing or preparing place, at times of triumphs. On the other side, which is the household side, I wish it divided at the first into a hall, and a chapel (with a partition between); both of good state, and bigness: and those not to go all the length, but to have, at the further end, a winter and a summer parlour, both fair. And under these rooms, a fair and large cellar, sunk under ground: and likewise, some privy kitchens, with butteries, and pantries, and the like. As for the tower, I would have it two storeys, of eighteen foot high a piece, above the two wings; and a goodly leads upon the top, railed with statues interposed; and the same tower to be divided into rooms, as shall be thought fit. The stairs likewise, to the upper rooms, let them be upon a fair open newel, and finely railed in, with images of wood, cast into a brass colour: and a very fair landing place at the top. But this to be, if you do not point any of the lower rooms, for a dining place of servants. For otherwise, you shall have the servants' dinner after your own: for the steam of it will come up as in a tunnel. And so much for the front. Only, I understand the height of the first stairs to be sixteen foot, which is the height of the lower room.

Beyond this front, is there to be a fair court, but three sides of it, of a far lower building than the front. And in all the four corners of that court, fair staircases, cast into turrets, on the outside, and not within the row of buildings themselves. But those towers are not to be of the height of the front; but rather proportionable to the lower building. Let the court not be paved, for that striketh up a great heat in summer, and much cold in winter. But only some side alleys, with a cross, and the quarters to graze, being kept shorn, but not too near shorn. The row of return, on the banquet side, let it be all stately galleries; in which galleries, let there be three or four fine cupolas, in the length of it, placed at equal distance: and fine coloured windows of several works. On the household side, chambers of presence, and ordinary entertainments, with some bed-chambers; and let all three sides be a double house, without through lights, on the sides, that you may have rooms from the sun, both for forenoon, and afternoon. Cast it also, that you may have rooms, both for summer, and winter: shady for summer, and warm for winter. You shall have sometimes fair houses, so full of glass, that one cannot tell where to become, to be out of the sun, or cold: for inbowed windows, I hold them of good use; (in cities indeed, upright do better, in respect of the uniformity towards the street;) for they be pretty retiring places for conference; and besides, they keep both the wind and sun off: for that which would strike almost through the room, doth scarce pass the window. But let them be but few, four in the court, on the sides only.

Beyond this court, let there be an inward court of the same square and height; which is to be environed, with the garden, on all sides: and in the inside, cloistered on all sides, upon decent and beautiful arches, as high as the first storey. On the under storey, towards the garden, let it be turned to a grotto, or place of shade, or estivation. And only have opening and windows towards the garden; and be level upon the floor, no whit sunk under ground, to avoid all dampishness. And let there be a fountain, or some fair work of statues, in the midst of this court; and to be paved as the other court was. These buildings to be for privy lodgings, on both sides; and the end, for privy galleries. Whereof, you must foresee, that one of them be for an infirmary, if the prince or any special person should be sick, with chambers, bed-chamber, antecamera, and recamera, joining to it. This upon the second storey. Upon the ground storey, a fair gallery, open, upon pillars: and upon the third storey likewise, an open gallery upon pillars, to take the prospect, and freshness of the garden. At both corners of the further side, by way of return, let there be two delicate or rich cabinets, daintily paved, richly hanged, glazed with crystalline glass, and a rich cupola in the midst; and all other elegancy that may be thought upon. In the upper gallery too, I wish that there may be, if the place will yield it, some fountains running, in divers places, from the wall, with some fine avoidances. And thus much, for the model of the palace: save that you must have, before you come to the front, three courts. A green court plain, with a wall about it: a second court of the same, but more garnished, with little turrets, or rather embellishments, upon the wall: and a third court, to make a square with the front, but not to be built, nor yet enclosed with a naked wall, but enclosed with terraces, leaded aloft, and fairly garnished, on the three sides; and cloistered on the inside, with pillars, and not with arches below. As for offices, let them stand at distance, with some lofty galleries, to pass from them to the palace itself.

46

Of Gardens

God Almighty first planted a garden. And indeed, it is the purest of human pleasure. It is the greatest refreshment to the spirits of man; without which buildings and palaces are but gross handy-works: and a man shall ever see, that when ages grow to civility and elegance, men come to build stately, sooner than to garden finely: as if gardening were the greater perfection. I do hold it, in the royal ordering of gardens, there ought to be gardens, for all the months in the year: in which, severally, things of beauty may be then in season. For December, and January, and the latter part of November, you must take such things as are green all winter: holly; ivy; bays; juniper; cypress trees; yew; pineapple trees; fir trees; rosemary; lavender; periwinkle, the white, the purple, and the blue; germander; flags; orange trees; lemon trees; and myrtles, if they be stoved; and sweet marjoram warm set. There followeth, for the latter part of January, and February, the mezereon tree, which then blossoms; *crocus vernus*, both the yellow, and the grey; primroses; anemones; the early tulip; *hyacinthus orientalis*; *chamairis*; *fritillaria*. For March, there come violets, specially the single blue, which are the earliest; the yellow daffodil; the daisy; the almond tree in blossom; the peach tree in blossom; the cornelian tree in blossom; sweet briar. In April follow, the double white violet; the wallflower; the stock gillyflower; the cowslip, fleur-de-lis, and lilies of [all] natures; rosemary flowers; the tulip; the double peony; the pale daffodil; the French honeysuckle; the cherry tree in blossom; the damson and plum trees in blossom; the white thorn in leaf; the lilac tree. In May and June, come pinks of all sorts, specially the blush pink; roses of all kinds, except the musk, which comes later; honeysuckles; strawberries; bugloss; columbine; the French marigold; *flos africanus*; cherry tree in fruit; *ribes*; figs in fruit;

raspberries; vine flowers; lavender in flowers; the sweet satyrian, with the white flower; *herba muscaria*; *lilium convallium*; the apple tree in blossom. In July, come gillyflowers of all varieties; musk roses; the lime tree in blossom; early pears, and plums in fruit; ginnitings; quadlins. In August, come plums of all sorts in fruit; pears; apricots; berberries; filberts; musk melons; monks-hoods, of all colours. In September, come grapes; apples; poppies of all colours; peaches; melo-cotones; nectarines; cornelians; wardens; quinces. In October, and the beginning of November, come services; medlars; bullises; roses cut or removed to come late; holly oaks; and such like. These particulars are for the climate of London; but my meaning is perceived, that you may have *ver perpetuum*, as the place affords.

And because the breath of flowers is far sweeter in the air (where it comes and goes, like the warbling of music) than in the hand, therefore nothing is more fit for that delight, than to know, what be the flowers, and plants that do best perfume the air. Roses, damask and red, are fast flowers of their smells; so that you may walk by a whole row of them, and find nothing of their sweetness; yea though it be in a morning's dew. Bays likewise yield no smell, as they grow. Rosemary little; nor sweet marjoram. That which above all others yields the sweetest smell in the air, is the violet; specially the white double violet, which comes twice a year; about the middle of April, and about Bartholomew-tide. Next to that is, the musk rose. Then the strawberry leaves dying, which [yield] a most excellent cordial smell. Then the flower of the vines; it is a little dust, like the dust of a bent, which grows upon the cluster, in the first coming forth. Then sweet briar. Then wallflowers, which are very delightful, to be set under a parlour, or lower chamber window. Then pinks, [and gillyflowers,] specially the matted pink, and clove gillyflower. Then the flowers of the lime tree. Then the honeysuckles, so they be somewhat a far off. Of bean flowers I speak not, because they are field flowers. But those which perfume the air most delightfully, not passed by as the rest, but being trodden upon and crushed, are three: that is burnet, wild thyme, and water mints. Therefore, you are to set whole alleys of them, to have the pleasure, when you walk or tread.

For gardens, (speaking of those, which are indeed princelike, as we have done of buildings) the contents ought not well to be under thirty acres of ground; and to be divided into three parts: a green in the entrance; a heath or desert in the going forth; and the [main] garden in the midst; besides alleys, on both sides. And I like well, that four acres of ground be assigned to the green; six to the heath; four and four to either side; and twelve to the main garden. The green hath two pleasures, the one, because nothing is more pleasant to the eye, than green grass kept finely shorn; the other, because it will give you a fair alley in the midst, by which you may go in front upon a stately hedge, which is to enclose the garden. But, because the alley will be long, and in great heat of the year, or day, you ought not to buy the shade, in the garden, by going in the sun through the green, therefore you are, of either side the green, to plant a covert alley, upon carpenter's work, about twelve foot in height, by which you may go in shade into the garden. As for the making of knots, or figures, with divers coloured earths, that they may lie under the windows of the house, on that side which the garden stands, they be but toys: you may see as good sights, many times, in tarts. The garden is best to be square; encompassed, on all the four sides, with a stately arched hedge. The arches to be upon pillars, of carpenter's work, of some ten foot high, and six foot broad: and the spaces between, of the same dimension, with the breadth of the arch. Over the arches, let there be an entire hedge, of some four foot high, framed also upon carpenter's work: and upon the upper hedge, over every arch, a little turret, with a belly, enough to receive a cage of birds: and over every space, between the arches, some other little figure, with broad plates of round coloured glass, gilt, for the sun to play upon. But this hedge I intend to be raised upon a bank, not steep, but gently slope, of some six foot, set all with flowers. Also I understand, that this square of the garden, should not be the whole breadth of the ground, but to leave, on either side, ground enough for diversity of side alleys: unto which, the two covert alleys of the green may deliver you. But there must be no alleys with hedges, at either end, of this great enclosure: not at the hither end, for letting your prospect upon this fair hedge from the green; nor at the further end, for letting your prospect from the hedge, through the arches, upon the heath.

For the ordering of the ground, within the great hedge, I leave it to variety of device; advising nevertheless, that whatsoever form you cast it into, first it be not too busy, or full of work. Wherein I, for my part, do not like images cut out in juniper, or other garden stuff: they be for children. Little low hedges, round, like welts, with some pretty pyramids, I like well: and in some places, fair columns upon frames of carpenter's work. I would also have the alleys spacious and fair. You may have closer alleys upon the side grounds but none in the main garden. I wish also, in the very middle, a fair mount, with three ascents, and alleys, enough for four to walk abreast; which I would have to be perfect circles, without any bulwarks, or embossment; and the whole mount, to be thirty foot high; and some fine banqueting house, with some chimneys neatly cast, and without too much glass.

For fountains, they are a great beauty, and refreshment; But pools mar all, and make the garden unwholesome, and full of flies, and frogs. Fountains I intend to be of two natures: the one, that sprinkleth or spouteth water; the other a fair receipt of water, of some thirty or forty foot square, but without fish, or slime, or mud. For the first, the ornaments of images gilt, or of marble, which are in use, do well: but the main matter is so to convey the water, as it never stay, either in the bowls, or in the cistern; that the water be never by rest discoloured, green, or red, or the like: or gather any mossiness or putrefaction. Besides that, it is to be cleansed every day by the hand. Also some steps up to it, and some fine pavement about it, doth well. As for the other kind of fountain, which we may call a bathing pool, it may admit much curiosity, and beauty; wherewith we will not trouble ourselves: as, that the bottom be finely paved, and with images: the sides likewise; and withal embellished with coloured glass, and such things of lustre; encompassed also, with fine rails of low statues. But the main point is the same, which we mentioned, in the former kind of fountain; which is, that the water be in perpetual motion, fed by a water higher than the pool and delivered into it by fair spouts, and then discharged away under ground, by some equality of bores, that it stay little. And for fine devices, of arching water without spilling, and making it rise in several forms (of feathers, drinking glasses, canopies, and the like), they be pretty things to look on, but nothing to health and sweetness.

For the heath, which was the third part of our plot, I wish it to be framed, as much as may be, to a natural wildness. Trees I would have none in it; but some thickets, made only of sweet-briar, and honeysuckle, and some wild vine amongst; and the ground set with violets, strawberries, and primroses. For these are sweet, and prosper in the shade. And these to be in the heath, here and there, not in any order. I like also little heaps, in the nature of mole-hills (such as are in wild heaths), to be set, some with wild thyme; some with pinks;

some with germander, that gives a good flower to the eye; some with periwinkles; some with violets; some with strawberries; some with cowslips; some with daisies; some with red roses; some with lilium convallium; some with sweet-williams red; some with bears-foot; and the like low flowers, being withal sweet, and sightly. Part of which heaps, to be with standards of little bushes, pricked upon their top, and part without. The standards to be roses; juniper; holly; berberries (but here and there, because of the smell of their blossom); red currants; gooseberries; rosemary; bays; sweet-briar; and such like. But these standards to be kept with cutting, that they grow not out of course.

For the side grounds, you are to fill them with variety of alleys, private, to give a full shade; some of them, wheresoever the sun be. You are to frame some of them likewise for shelter, that when the wind blows sharp, you may walk, as in a gallery. And those alleys must be likewise hedged, at both ends, to keep out the wind; and these closer alleys, must be ever finely gravelled, and no grass, because of going wet. In many of these alleys likewise, you are to set fruit trees of all sorts; as well upon the walls, as in ranges. And this would be generally observed, that the borders, wherein you plant your fruit trees, be fair and large, and low, and not steep; and set with fine flowers, but thin and sparingly, lest they deceive trees. At the end of both the side grounds, I would have a mount of some pretty height, leaving the wall of the enclosure, breast high, to look abroad into the fields.

For the main garden, I do not deny, but there should be some fair alleys, ranged on both sides, with fruit trees; and some pretty tufts of fruit trees, and arbours with seats, set in some decent order; but these to be by no means set too thick; but to leave the main garden, so as it be not close, but the air open and free. For as for shade, I would have you rest upon the alleys of the side grounds, there to walk, if you be disposed, in the heat of the year, or day; but to make account, that the main garden is for the more temperate parts of the year; and in the heat of summer, for the morning, and the evening, or over-cast days.

For aviaries, I like them not, except they be of that largeness, as they may be turfed, and have living plants, and bushes, set in them; that the birds may have more scope, and natural nesting, and that no foulness appear in the floor of the aviary. So I have made a platform of a princely garden, partly by precept, partly by drawing, not a model, but some general lines of it; and in this I have spared for no cost. But it is nothing for great princes, that for the most part, taking advice with workmen, with no less cost, set their things together; and sometimes add statues, and such things, for state, and magnificence, but nothing to the true pleasure of a garden.

47

Of Negotiating

It is generally better to deal by speech, than by letter; and by the mediation of a third, than by a man's self. Letters are good, when a man would draw an answer by letter back again; or when it may seem, for a man's justification, afterwards to produce his own letter; or where it may be danger to be interrupted, or heard by pieces. To deal in person is good, when a man's face breedeth regard, as commonly with inferiors; or in tender cases, where a man's eye, upon the countenance of him with whom he speaketh, may give him a direction, how far to go: and generally, where a man will reserve to himself liberty either to disavow, or to expound. In choice of instruments, it is better to choose men of a plainer sort, that are like to do that, that is committed to them, and to report back again faithfully the success; than those, that are cunning to contrive out of other men's business, somewhat to grace themselves; and will help the matter, in report, for satisfaction sake. Use also such persons as affect the business, wherein they are employed; for that quickeneth much; and such as are fit for the matter; as bold men for expostulation, fair spoken men for persuasion, crafty men for enquiry and observation, froward and absurd men for business that doth not well bear out itself. Use also such as have been lucky, and prevailed before in things wherein you have employed them; for that breeds confidence, and they will strive to maintain their prescription. It is better to sound a person, with whom one deals, a far off, than to fall upon the point at first; except you mean to surprise him by some short question. It is better dealing with men in appetite, than with those that are where they would be. If a man deal with another upon conditions, the start or first performance is all; which a man cannot reasonably demand, except either the nature of the thing be such, which must go before;

or else a man can persuade the other party, that he shall still need him, in some other thing; or else that he be counted the honester man. All practice is to discover, or to work. Men discover themselves, in trust; in passion; at unawares; and of necessity, when they would have somewhat done, and cannot find an apt pretext. If you would work any man, you must either know his nature, and fashions, and so lead him; or his ends, and so persuade him; or his weakness, and disadvantages, and so awe him; or those that have interest in him, and so govern him. In dealing with cunning persons, we must ever consider their ends, to interpret their speeches; and it is good to say little to them, and that which they least look for. In all negotiations of difficulty, a man may not look to sow and reap at once; but must prepare business, and so ripen it by degrees.

48

Of Followers & Friends

Costly followers are not to be liked; lest while a man maketh his train longer, he make his wings shorter. I reckon to be costly, not them alone, which charge the purse, but which are wearisome and importune in suits. Ordinary followers ought to challenge no higher conditions, than countenance, recommendation, and protection from wrongs. Factious followers are worse to be liked, which follow not upon affection to him, with whom they range themselves, but upon discontentment conceived against some other: whereupon commonly ensueth that ill intelligence, that we many times see between great personages. Likewise glorious followers, who make themselves as trumpets, of the commendation of those they follow, are full of inconvenience; for they taint business through want of secrecy; and they export honour from a man, and make him a return in envy. There is a kind of followers likewise, which are dangerous, being indeed espials; which enquire the secrets of the house, and bear tales of them to others. Yet such men, many times, are in great favour; for they are officious, and commonly exchange tales. The following by certain estates of men, answerable to that which a great person himself professeth (as of soldiers to him that hath been employed in the wars, and the like), hath ever been a thing civil, and well taken even in monarchies; so it be without too much pomp or popularity. But the most honourable kind of following, is to be followed as one that apprehendeth, to advance virtue and desert, in all sorts of persons. And yet, where there is no eminent odds in sufficiency, it is better to take with the more passable, than with the more able. And besides, to speak truth, in base times, active men are of more use, than virtuous. It is true that in government, it is good to use men of one rank equally: for to countenance some extraordinarily, is to make them insolent, and the rest discontent; because they may claim a due. But contrariwise in favour, to use men with much difference and election, is good; for it maketh the persons preferred more thankful, and the rest more officious; because all is of favour. It is good discretion, not to make too much of any man, at the first; because one cannot hold out that proportion. To be governed (as we call it) by one, is not safe: for it shows softness, and gives a freedom to scandal and disreputation: for those that would not censure, or speak ill of a man immediately, will talk more boldly of those that are so great with them, and thereby wound their honour. Yet to be distracted with many is worse; for it makes men to be of the last impression, and full of change. To take advice of some few friends is ever honourable; for lookers-on, many times, see more than game-sters; and the vale best discovereth the hill. There is little friendship in the world, and least of all between equals, which was wont to be magnified. That that is, is between superior and inferior, whose fortunes may comprehend, the one the other.

49

Of Suitors

Many ill matters and projects are undertaken; and private suits do putrefy the public good. Many good matters are undertaken with bad minds; I mean not only corrupt minds, but crafty minds, that intend not performance. Some embrace suits, which never mean to deal effectually in them; but if they see there may be life in the matter, by some other mean, they will be content to win a thank, or take a second reward, or at least to make use, in the mean time, of the suitor's hopes. Some take hold of suits only for an occasion, to cross some other; or to make an information, whereof they could not otherwise have apt pretext; without care what become of the suit, when that turn is served: or generally, to make other men's business a kind of entertainment, to bring in their own. Nay, some undertake suits with a full purpose, to let them fall; to the end, to gratify the adverse party, or competitor. Surely, there is, in some sort, a right in every suit: either a right of equity, if it be a suit of controversy; or a right of desert, if it be a suit of petition. If affection lead a man to favour the wrong side in justice, let him rather use his countenance to compound the matter, than to carry it. If affection lead a man to favour the less worthy in desert, let him do it without depraving or disabling the better deserver. In suits, which a man doth not well understand, it is good to refer them to some friend of trust and judgement, that may report whether he may deal in them with honour: but let him choose well his referendaries, for else he may be led by the nose. Suitors are so distasted with delays, and abuses, that plain dealing, in denying to deal in suits at first, and reporting the success barely, and in challenging no more thanks than one hath deserved, is grown not only honourable, but also gracious. In suits of favour, the first coming ought to take little place: so far forth consideration may be had of his trust, that if intelligence of the matter could not otherwise have been had, but by him, advantage be not taken of the note, but the party left to his other means; and, in some sort, recompensed for his discovery. To be ignorant of the value of a suit, is simplicity; as well as to be ignorant of the right thereof, is want of conscience. Secrecy in suits is a great mean of obtaining; for voicing them, to be in forwardness, may discourage some kind of suitors; but doth quicken and awake others. But timing of the suit is the principal. Timing, I say, not only in respect of the person that should grant it, but in respect of those which are like to cross it. Let a man, in the choice of his mean, rather choose the fittest mean, than the greatest mean: and rather them, that deal in certain things, than those that are general. The reparation of a denial is sometimes equal to the first grant; if a man show himself neither dejected, nor discontented. *Iniquum petas, ut aequum feras*; is a good rule, where a man hath strength of favour: but otherwise, a man were better rise in his suit; for he that would have ventured at first to have lost the suitor, will not in the conclusion lose both the suitor, and his own former favour. Nothing is thought so basic a request, to a great person, as his letter; and yet, if it be not in a good cause, it is so much out of his reputation. There are no worse instruments, than these general contrivers of suits: for they are but a kind of poison and infection to public proceedings.

50

Of Studies

Studies serve for delight, for ornament, and for ability. Their chief use
for delight, is in privateness and retiring; for ornament, is in discourse;
and for ability, is in the judgement and disposition of business. For
expert men can execute, and perhaps judge of particulars, one by one;
but the general counsels, and the plots, and marshalling of affairs,
come best from those that are learned. To spend too much time in
studies, is sloth; to use them too much for ornament, is affectation; to
make judgement wholly by their rules is the humour of a scholar.
They perfect nature, and are perfected by experience: for natural
abilities are like natural plants, that need pruning by study: and studies
themselves do give forth directions too much at large, except they be
bounded in by experience. Crafty men condemn studies; simple men
admire them; and wise men use them: for they teach not their own
use; but that is a wisdom without them, and above them, won by
observation. Read not to contradict, and confute; nor to believe and
take for granted; nor to find talk and discourse; but to weigh and
consider. Some books are to be tasted, others to be swallowed, and
some few to be chewed and digested: that is, some books are to be
read only in parts; others to be read but not curiously; and some few
to be read wholly, and with diligence and attention. Some books also
may be read by deputy, and extracts made of them by others: but that
would be, only in the less important arguments, and the meaner sort
of book: else distilled books are like common distilled waters, flashy
things. Reading maketh a full man; conference a ready man; and
writing an exact man. And therefore, if a man write little, he had
need have a great memory; if he confer little, he had need have a
present wit; and if he read little, he had need have much cunning, to
seem to know that he doth not. Histories make men wise; poets

witty; the mathematics subtle; natural philosophy deep; moral grave; logic and rhetoric able to contend. *Abeunt studia in mores*. Nay, there is no stond or impediment in the wit, but may be wrought out by fit studies: like as diseases of the body may have appropriate exercises. Bowling is good for the stone and reins; shooting for the lungs and breast; gentle walking for the stomach; riding for the head; and the like. So if a man's wit be wandering, let him study the mathematics; for in demonstrations, if his wit be called away never so little, he must begin again: if his wit be not apt to distinguish or find differences, let him study the schoolmen; for they are *cymini sectores*. If he be not apt to beat over matters, and to call up one thing, to prove and illustrate another, let him study the lawyers' cases: so every defect of the mind may have a special receipt.

51

Of Faction

Many have an opinion not wise, that for a prince to govern his estate, or for a great person to govern his proceedings, according to the respect of factions, is a principal part of policy: whereas contrariwise, the chiefest wisdom is, either in ordering those things which are general, and wherein men of several factions do nevertheless agree; or in dealing with correspondence to particular persons, one by one. But I say not, that the consideration of factions is to be neglected. Mean men, in their rising, must adhere; but great men, that have strength in themselves, were better to maintain themselves indifferent, and neutral. Yet even in beginners, to adhere so moderately, as he be a man of the one faction, which is most passable with the other, commonly giveth best way. The lower and weaker faction is the firmer in conjunction: and it is often seen, that a few that are stiff, do tire out a greater number that are more moderate. When one of the factions is extinguished, the remaining subdivideth: as the faction, between Lucullus and the rest of the nobles of the Senate (which they called *Optimates*) held out a while, against the faction of Pompey and Caesar: but when the senate's authority was ruled down, Caesar and Pompey soon after brake. The faction or party of Antonius, and Octavianus Caesar, against Brutus and Cassius, held out likewise for a time: but when Brutus and Cassius were overthrown, then soon after Antonius and Octavianus brake and subdivided. These examples are of wars, but the same holdeth in private factions. And therefore, those that are seconds in factions do many times, when the faction subdivideth, prove principals: but many times also, they prove ciphers and cashiered: for many a man's strength is in opposition; and when that faileth, he groweth out of use. It is commonly seen, that men once placed, take in with the contrary faction to that by which they enter; thinking belike that they have the first sure; and now are ready for a new purchase. The traitor in faction lightly goeth away with it; for when matters have stuck long in balancing, the winning of some one man casteth them, and he getteth all the thanks. The even carriage between two factions proceedeth not always of moderation, but of a trueness to a man's self, with end to make use of both. Certainly in Italy, they hold it a little suspect in Popes, when they have often in their mouth, *padre commune*: and take it to be a sign of one, that meaneth to refer all to the greatness of his own house. Kings had need beware how they side themselves, and make themselves as of a faction or party: for leagues within the state are ever pernicious to monarchies; for they raise an obligation, paramount to obligation of sovereignty, and make the king *tanquam unus ex nobis*: as was to be seen in the league of France. When factions are carried too high, and too violently, it is a sign of weakness in princes; and much to the prejudice, both of their authority, and business. The motions of factions, under kings, ought to be like the motions (as the astronomers speak) of the inferior orbs; which may have their proper motions, but yet still, are quietly carried by the higher motion of *primum mobile*.

52

Of Ceremonies & Respects

He that is only real, had need have exceeding great parts of virtue: as the stone had need to be rich, that is set without foil. But if a man mark it well, it is in praise and commendation of men as it is in gettings and gains: for the proverb is true, that light gains make heavy purses; for light gains come thick, whereas great come but now and then. So it is true, that small matters win great commendation, because they are continually in use, and in note: whereas the occasion of any great virtue cometh but on festivals. Therefore it doth much add to a man's reputation, and is (as Queen Isabella said) like perpetual letters commendatory, to have good forms. To attain them, it almost sufficeth, not to despise them: for so shall a man observe them in others: and let him trust himself with the rest. For if he labour too much to express them, he shall lose their grace; which is to be natural and unaffected. Some men's behaviour is like a verse, wherein every syllable is measured: how can a man comprehend great matters, that breaketh his mind too much to small observations? Not to use ceremonies at all, is to teach others not to use them again; and so diminisheth respect to himself: especially they be not to be omitted to strangers, and formal natures: but the dwelling upon them, and exalting them above the moon, is not only tedious, but doth diminish the faith and credit of him that speaks. And certainly, there is a kind of conveying of effectual and imprinting passages, amongst compliments, which is of singular use, if a man can hit upon it. Amongst a man's peers, a man shall be sure of familiarity; and therefore, it is good a little to keep state. Amongst a man's inferiors, one shall be sure of reverence; and therefore it is good a little to be familiar. He that is too much in anything, so that he giveth another occasion of satiety, maketh himself cheap. To apply one's self to others is good: so it be with demonstration, that a man doth it upon regard and not upon facility. It is a good precept, generally in seconding another, yet to add somewhat of one's own: as if you will grant his opinion, let it be with some distinction; if you will follow his motion, let it be with condition; if you allow his counsel, let it be with alleging further reason. Men had need beware, how they be too perfect in compliments; for be they never so sufficient otherwise, their enviers will be sure to give them that attribute, to the disadvantage of their greater virtues. It is loss also in business, to be too full of respects, or to be too curious in observing times and opportunities. Solomon saith; He that considereth the wind shall not sow, and he that looketh to the clouds shall not reap. A wise man will make more opportunities than he finds. Men's behaviour should be like their apparel, not too strait, or point device, but free for exercise or motion.

53

Of Praise

Praise is the reflection of virtue. But it is as the glass or body, which giveth the reflection. If it be from the common people, it is commonly false and naught: and rather followeth vain persons, than virtuous: for the common people understand not many excellent virtues: the lowest virtues draw praise from them; the middle virtues work in them astonishment, or admiration; but of the highest virtues, they have no sense or perceiving at all. But shows, and *species virtutibus similes*, serve best with them. Certainly, fame is like a river, that beareth up things light and swollen, and drowns things weighty and solid: but if persons of quality and judgement concur, then it is, (as the scripture saith) *nomen bonum instar unguenti fragrantis*. It filleth all round about, and will not easily away. For the odours of ointments are more durable, than those of flowers. There be so many false points of praise, that a man may justly hold it a suspect. Some praises proceed merely of flattery; and if he be an ordinary flatterer, he will have certain common attributes, which may serve every man; if he be a cunning flatterer, he will follow the arch-flatterer, which is a man's self; and wherein a man thinketh that of himself, therein the flatterer will uphold him most; but if he be an impudent flatterer, look wherein a man is conscious to himself that he is most defective, and is most out of countenance in himself, that will the flatterer entitle him to, perforce, *spreta conscientia*. Some praises come of good wishes, and respects, which is a form due in civility to kings, and great persons, *laudando praecipere*; when by telling men what they are, they represent to them what they should be. Some men are praised maliciously to their hurt, thereby to stir envy and jealousy towards them; *pessimum genus inimicorum laudantium*; in so much as it was a proverb, amongst the Grecians; that, he that was praised to his hurt, should have a push rise upon his nose: as we say; that a blister will rise upon one's tongue, that tells a lie. Certainly moderate praise, used with opportunity, and not vulgar, is that which doth the good. Solomon saith, He that praiseth his friend aloud, rising early, it shall be to him no better than a curse. Too much magnifying of man or matter doth irritate contradiction, and procure envy and scorn. To praise a man's self cannot be decent, except it be in rare cases: but to praise a man's office or profession, he may do it with good grace, and with a kind of magnanimity. The cardinals of Rome, which are theologues, and friars, and schoolmen, have a phrase of notable contempt and scorn towards civil business: for they call all temporal business, of wars, embassages, judicature, and other employments, *sbirrerie*; which is, under-sheriffries; as if they were but matters for under-sheriffs and catchpoles; though many times, those under-sheriffries do more good than their high speculations. St Paul, when he boasts of himself, he doth oft interlace; I speak like a fool; but speaking of his calling, he saith; *magnificabo apostolatum meum*.

54

Of Vainglory

It was prettily devised of Aesop; the fly sat upon the axle-tree of the chariot wheel, and said, What a dust do I raise? So are there some vain persons, that whatsoever goeth alone, or moveth upon greater means, if they have never so little hand in it, they think it is they that carry it. They that are glorious, must needs be factious; for all bravery stands upon comparisons. They must needs be violent, to make good their own vaunts. Neither can they be secret, and therefore not effectual; but according to the French proverb; *beaucoup de bruit, peu de fruit*: much bruit, little fruit. Yet certainly there is use of this quality, in civil affairs. Where there is an opinion, and fame to be created, either of virtue, or greatness, these men are good trumpeters. Again, as Titus Livius noteth, in the case of Antiochus, and the Aetolians; there are sometimes great effects of cross lies; as if a man that negotiates between two princes, to draw them to join in a war against the third, doth extol the forces of either of them above measure, the one to the other: and sometimes, he that deals between man and man, raiseth his own credit with both by pretending greater interest, than he hath in either. And in these, and the like kinds, it often falls out that somewhat is produced of nothing: for lies are sufficient to breed opinion, and opinion brings on substance. In military commanders and soldiers, vainglory is an essential point; for as iron sharpens iron, so by glory one courage sharpeneth another. In cases of great enterprise, upon charge and adventure, a composition of glorious natures doth put life into business; and those that are of solid and sober natures have more of the ballast, than of the sail. In fame of learning, the flight will be slow, without some feathers of ostentation. *Qui de contemnenda gloria libros scribunt, nomen suum inscribunt.* Socrates, Aristotle, Galen, were men full of ostentation. Certainly vainglory helpeth to perpetuate a man's memory; and virtue was never so beholding to human nature, as it received his due at the second hand. Neither had the fame of Cicero, Seneca, Plinius Secundus, borne her age so well, if it had not been joined with some vanity in themselves: like unto varnish, that makes sealings not only shine, but last. But all this while, when I speak of vainglory, I mean not of that property, that Tacitus doth attribute to Mucianus; *omnium, quae dixerat feceratque, arte quadam ostentator*: for that proceeds not of vanity, but of natural magnanimity, and discretion: and in some persons is not only comely, but gracious. For excusations, cessions, modesty itself well governed, are but arts of ostentation. And amongst those arts there is none better, than that which Plinius Secundus speaketh of; which is to be liberal of praise and commendation to others, in that wherein a man's self hath any perfection. For saith Pliny very wittily; In commending another, you do your self right; for he that you commend, is either superior to you, in that you commend, or inferior. If he be inferior, if he be to be commended, you much more: if he be superior, if he be not to be commended, you much less. Glorious men are the scorn of wise men; the admiration of fools; the idols of parasites; and the slaves of their own vaunts.

55

Of Honour & Reputation

The winning of honour is but the revealing of a man's virtue and worth, without disadvantage. For some in their actions do woo and affect honour and reputation. Which sort of men are commonly much talked of, but inwardly little admired. And some, contrariwise, darken their virtue, in the show of it; so as they be undervalued in opinion. If a man perform that which hath not been attempted before; or attempted and given over; or hath been achieved, but not with so good circumstance; he shall purchase more honour, than by effecting a matter of greater difficulty, or virtue, wherein he is but a follower. If a man so temper his actions, as in some one of them he doth content every faction, or combination of people, the music will be the fuller. A man is an ill husband of his honour, that entereth into any action, the failing wherein may disgrace him more, than the carrying of it through can honour him. Honour that is gained and broken upon another, hath the quickest reflection; like diamonds cut with facets. And therefore, let a man contend to excel any competitors of his in honour, in out-shooting them, if he can, in their own bow. Discreet followers and servants help much to reputation. *Omnis fama a domesticis emanat*. Envy, which is the canker of honour, is best extinguished by declaring a man's self in his ends, rather to seek merit, than fame: and by attributing a man's successes, rather to divine providence and felicity, than to his own virtue or policy. The true marshalling of the degrees of sovereign honour are these. In the first place are *conditores imperiorum*; founders of states, and commonwealths: such as were Romulus, Cyrus, Caesar, Ottoman, Ismael. In the second place are *legislatores*, lawgivers; which are also called, second founders, or *perpetui principes*, because they govern by their ordinances, after they are gone: such were Lycurgus, Solon, Justinian,

Eadgar, Alphonsus of Castile, the Wise, that made the *Siete Partidas*. In the third place are *liberatores*, or *salvatores*: such as compound the long miseries of civil wars, or deliver their countries from servitude of strangers or tyrants; as Augustus Caesar, Vespasianus, Aurelianus, Theodoricus, Henry VII of England and Henry IV of France. In the fourth place are *propagatores* or *propugnatores imperii*; such as in honourable wars enlarge their territories, or make noble defence against invaders. And in the last place are *patres patriae*; which reign justly, and make the times good, wherein they live. Both which last kinds need no examples, they are in such number. Degrees of honour in subjects are; first, *participes curarum*; those upon whom princes do discharge the greatest weight of their affairs; their right hands, as we call them. The next are *duces belli*, great leaders; such as are princes' lieutenants, and do them notable services in the wars. The third are *gratiosi*, favourites; such as exceed not this scantling; to be solace to the sovereign, and harmless to the people. And the fourth, *negotiis pares*; such as have great places under princes, and execute their places with sufficiency. There is an honour likewise, which may be ranked amongst the greatest, which happeneth rarely: that is, of such as sacrifice themselves, to death or danger, for the good of their country: as was M. Regulus, and the two Decii.

56

Of Judicature

Judges ought to remember, that their office is *ius dicere*, and not *ius dare*; to interpret law, and not to make law, or give law. Else will it be like the authority claimed by the church of Rome; which under pretext of exposition of scripture, doth not stick to add and alter; and to pronounce that which they do not find; and by show of antiquity, to introduce novelty. Judges ought to be more learned, than witty; more reverent, than plausible; and more advised, than confident. Above all things, integrity is their portion, and proper virtue. Cursed (saith the law) is he that removeth the landmark. The mislayer of a mere stone is to blame. But it is the unjust judge that is the capital remover of landmarks, when he defineth amiss of lands and property. One foul sentence doth more hurt, than many foul examples. For these do but corrupt the stream; the other corrupteth the fountain. So saith Solomon; *Fons turbatus, et vena corrupta, est iustus cadens in causa sua coram adversario*. The office of judges may have reference unto the parties that sue; unto the advocates that plead; unto the clerks and ministers of justice underneath them and to the sovereign or state above them.

First, for the causes or parties that sue. There be (saith the scripture) that turn judgement into wormwood; and surely, there be also, that turn it into vinegar; for injustice maketh it bitter, and delays make it sour. The principal duty of a judge is to suppress force and fraud; whereof force is the more pernicious, when it is open; and fraud, when it is close and disguised. Add thereto contentious suits, which ought to be spewed out, as the surfeit of courts. A judge ought to prepare his way to a just sentence, as God useth to prepare his way, by raising valleys, and taking down hills: so when there appeareth on either side, an high hand, violent prosecution, cunning advantages taken, combination, power, great counsel, then is the virtue of a judge seen, to make inequality equal; that he may plant his judgement, as upon an even ground. *Qui fortiter emungit, elicit sanguinem*; and where the winepress is hard wrought, it yields a harsh wine, that tastes of the grapestone. Judges must beware of hard constructions, and strained inferences; for there is no worse torture, than the torture of laws. Specially in case of laws penal, they ought to have care, that that which was meant for terror be not turned into rigour; and that they bring not upon the people that shower, whereof the scripture speaketh; *pluet super eos laqueos*: for penal laws pressed, are a shower of snares upon the people. Therefore, let penal laws, if they have been sleepers of long, or if they be grown unfit for the present time, be by wise judges confined in the execution; *iudicis officium est, ut res, ita tempora rerum, &c.* In causes of life and death; judges ought (as far as the law permitteth) in justice to remember mercy; and to cast a severe eye upon the example, but a merciful eye upon the person.

Secondly, for the advocates and counsel that plead: patience and gravity of hearing is an essential part of justice; and an overspeaking judge is no well tuned cymbal. It is no grace to a judge, first to find that which he might have heard, in due time, from the bar; or to show quickness of conceit in cutting off evidence or counsel too short; or to prevent information, by questions though pertinent. The parts of a judge in hearing are four: to direct the evidence; to moderate length, repetition, or impertinency of speech; to recapitulate, select, and collate the material points of that which hath been said; and to give the rule or sentence. Whatsoever is above these, is too much; and proceedeth, either of glory and willingness to speak; or of impatience to hear; or of shortness of memory; or of want of a staid and equal attention. It is a strange thing to see, that the boldness of advocates should prevail with judges; whereas they should imitate God, in whose seat they sit; who represseth the presumptuous, and giveth grace to the modest. But it is more strange, that judges should have noted favourites; which cannot but cause multiplication of fees, and suspicion of byways. There is due from the judge, to the advocate, some commendation and gracing, where causes are well handled, and fair pleaded; especially towards the side which obtaineth not; for that upholds, in the client, the reputation of his counsel, and beats down, in him, the conceit of his cause. There is likewise due to the public a civil reprehension of advocates, where there appeareth cunning counsel, gross neglect, slight information, indiscreet pressing, or an over-bold defence. And let not the counsel at the bar chop with the judge, nor wind himself into the handling of the cause anew, after the judge hath declared his sentence: but on the other side, let not the judge meet the cause half way; nor give occasion to the party to say; his counsel or proofs were not heard.

Thirdly, for that that concerns clerks, and ministers. The place of justice is an hallowed place; and therefore, not only the bench, but the footpace, and precincts, and purprise thereof, ought to be preserved without scandal and corruption. For certainly, graves (as the scripture saith) will not be gathered of thorns or thistles: neither can justice yield her fruit with sweetness, amongst the briars and brambles, of catching and polling clerks and ministers. The attendance of courts is subject to four bad instruments. First, certain persons that are the sowers of suits; which make the court swell, and the country pine. The second sort is of those that engage courts in quarrels of jurisdiction, and are not truly *amici curiae*, but *parasiti curiae*; in puffing a court up beyond her bounds, for their own scraps, and advantage. The third sort is of those that may be accounted the left hands of courts; persons that are full of nimble and sinister tricks and shifts, whereby they pervert the plain and direct courses of courts, and bring justice into oblique lines and labyrinths. And the fourth is, the poller and exacter of fees; which justifies the common resemblance of the courts of justice to the bush, whereunto while the sheep flies for defence in weather, he is sure to lose part of his fleece. On the other side, an ancient clerk, skilful in precedents, wary in proceeding, and understanding in the business of the court, is an excellent finger of a court; and doth many times point the way to the judge himself.

Fourthly, for that which may concern the sovereign and estate. Judges ought above all to remember the conclusion of the Roman twelve tables; *salus populi suprema lex*; and to know that laws, except they be in order to that end, are but things captious, and oracles not well inspired. Therefore it is an happy thing in a state, when kings and states do often consult with judges; and again, when judges do often consult with the king and state: the one, when there is matter of law, intervenient in business of state; the other, when there is some consideration of state, intervenient in matter of law. For many times, the things deduced to judgement may be *meum and tuum*, when the reason and consequence thereof may trench to point of estate: I call matter of estate, not only the parts of sovereignty, but whatsoever introduceth any great alteration, or dangerous precedent; or concerneth manifestly any great portion of people. And let no man weakly conceive that just laws, and true policy, have any antipathy: for they are like the spirits, and sinews, that one moves with the other. Let judges also remember, that Solomon's throne was supported by lions, on both sides; let them be lions, but yet lions under the throne; being circumspect, that they do not check or oppose any points of sovereignty. Let not judges also be so ignorant of their own right, as to think there is not left to them, as a principal part of their office, a wise use, and application of laws. For they may remember, what the apostle saith, of a greater law than theirs; *nos scimus quia lex bona est, modo quis ea utatur legitime.*

57

Of Anger

To seek to extinguish anger utterly, is but a bravery of the Stoics. We have better oracles: Be angry, but sin not. Let not the sun go down upon your anger. Anger must be limited, and confined, both in race, and in time. We will first speak, how the natural inclination, and habit, to be angry, may be attempered, and calmed. Secondly, how the particular motions of anger may be repressed, or at least refrained from doing mischief. Thirdly, how to raise anger, or appease anger, in another.

For the first; there is no other way, but to meditate and ruminate well upon the effects of anger, how it troubles man's life. And the best time to do this, is to look back upon anger, when the fit is thoroughly over. Seneca saith well; that anger is like ruin, which forsakes itself upon that it falls. The scripture exhorteth us; to possess our souls in patience. Whosoever is out of patience, is out of possession of his soul. Men must not turn bees;

animasque in vulnere ponunt.

Anger is certainly a kind of baseness: as it appears well, in the weakness of those subjects, in whom it reigns; children, women, old folks, sick folks. Only men must beware, that they carry their anger rather with scorn, than with fear: so that they may seem rather to be above the injury, than below it: which is a thing easily done, if a man will give law to himself in it.

For the second point; the causes and motives of anger, are chiefly three. First, to be too sensible of hurt: for no man is angry, that feels not himself hurt: and therefore tender and delicate persons must needs be oft angry: they have so many things to trouble them; which more robust natures have little sense of. The next is, the apprehension and construction of the injury offered, to be, in the circumstances thereof, full of contempt. For contempt is that which putteth an edge upon anger, as much, or more, than the hurt itself. And therefore, when men are ingenious in picking out circumstances of contempt, they do kindle their anger much. Lastly, opinion of the touch of a man's reputation doth multiply and sharpen anger. Wherein the remedy is, that a man should have, as Consalvo was wont to say, *telam honoris crassiorem*. But in all refrainings of anger, it is the best remedy to win time; and to make a man's self believe, that the opportunity of his revenge is not yet come: but that he foresees a time for it; and so to still himself in the mean time, and reserve it.

To continue anger from mischief, though it take hold of a man, there be two things whereof you must have special caution. The one, of extreme bitterness of words; especially, if they be accurate, and proper: for *communia maledicta* are nothing so much: and again, that in anger, a man reveal no secrets: for that makes him not fit for society. The other, that you do not peremptorily break off, in any business, in a fit of anger: but howsoever you show bitterness, do not act anything that is not revocable.

For raising and appeasing anger in another; it is done chiefly by choosing of times. When men are frowardest and worst disposed, to incense them. Again, by gathering (as was touched before) all that you can find out, to aggravate the contempt. And the two remedies are by the contraries. The former, to take good times, when first to relate to a man an angry business: for the first impression is much. And the other is, to sever, as much as may be, the construction of the injury from the point of contempt: imputing it to misunderstanding, fear, passion, or what you will.

58

Of Vicissitude of Things

Solomon saith; There is no new thing upon the earth. So that as Plato had an imagination, that all knowledge was but remembrance: so Solomon giveth his sentence, that all novelty is but oblivion. Whereby you may see, that the river of Lethe runneth as well above ground, as below. There is an abstruse astrologer that saith; If it were not for two things, that are constant (the one is, that the fixed stars ever stand at like distance, one from another, and never come nearer together, nor go further asunder; the other, that the diurnal motion perpetually keepeth time); no individual would last one moment. Certain it is, that the matter is in a perpetual flux, and never at a stay. The great winding-sheets, that bury all things in oblivion, are two; deluges, and earthquakes. As for conflagrations, and great droughts, they do not merely dispeople, and destroy. Phaeton's car went but a day. And the three years' drought, in the time of Elias, was but particular, and left people alive. As for the great burnings by lightnings, which are often in the West Indies, they are but narrow. But in the other two destructions, by deluge, and earthquake, it is further to be noted, that the remnant of people which hap to be preserved, are commonly ignorant and mountainous people, that can give no account of the time past: so that the oblivion is all one, as if none had been left. If you consider well, of the people of the West Indies, it is very probable that they are newer or a younger people, than the people of the old world. And it is much more likely, that the destruction that hath heretofore been there, was not by earthquakes (as the Egyptian priest told Solon, concerning the Island of Atlantis; that it was swallowed by an earthquake), but rather, that it was desolated by a particular deluge. For earthquakes are seldom in those parts. But on the other side, they have such pouring rivers, as the rivers of Asia and Africa and Europe are but brooks to them. Their Andes likewise, or mountains, are far higher than those with us; whereby it seems that the remnants of generation of men were, in such a particular deluge, saved. As for the observation, that Macbeth hath, that the jealousies of sects doth much extinguish the memory of things; traducing Gregory the Great, that he did what in him lay, to extinguish all heathen antiquities; I do not find that those zeals do any great effects, nor last long: as it appeared in the succession of Sabinian, who did revive the former antiquities.

The vicissitudes or mutations in the superior globe, are no fit matter for this present argument. It may be, Plato's great year, if the world should last so long, would have some effect; not in renewing the state of like individuals (for that is the fume of those that conceive the celestial bodies have more accurate influences upon these things below, than indeed they have), but in gross. Comets, out of question, have likewise power and effect, over the gross and mass things: but they are rather gazed upon, and waited upon in their journey, than wisely observed in their effects; specially in their respective effects; that is, what kind of comet, for magnitude, colour, version of the beams, placing in the region of heaven, or lasting, produceth what kind of effects

There is a toy which I have heard, and I would not have it given over, but waited upon a little. They say, it is observed in the Low Countries (I know not in what part) that every five and thirty years, the same kind and suit of years and weathers comes about again: as great frosts, great wet, great droughts, warm winters, summers with little heat, and the like: and they call it the prime. It is a thing I do the rather mention, because computing backwards, I have found some concurrence.

But to leave these points of nature, and to come to men. The greatest vicissitude of things amongst men, is the vicissitude of sects and religions. For those orbs rule in men's minds most. The true religion is built upon the rock; the rest are tossed upon the waves of time. To speak therefore, of the causes of new sects; and to give some counsel concerning them; as far as the weakness of human judgement, can give stay to so great revolutions.

When the religion formerly received is rent by discords; and when the holiness of the professors of religion is decayed, and full of scandal; and withal the times be stupid, ignorant, and barbarous; you may doubt the springing up of a new sect; if then also there should arise any extravagant and strange spirit, to make himself author thereof. All which points held, when Mohammed published his law. If a new sect have not two properties, fear it not: for it will not spread. The one is, the supplanting, or the opposing, of authority established: for nothing is more popular than that. The other is, the giving licence to pleasures, and a voluptuous life. For as for speculative heresies (such as were in ancient times the Arians, and now the Armenians) though they work mightily upon men's wits, yet they do not produce any great alterations in states; except it be by the help of civil occasions. There be three manner of plantations of new sects. By the power of signs and miracles: by the eloquence and wisdom of speech and persuasion: and by the sword. For martyrdoms, I reckon them amongst miracles; because they seem to exceed the strength of human nature: and I may do the like of superlative and admirable holiness of life. Surely, there is no better way to stop the rising of new sects, and schisms; than to reform abuses; to compound the smaller differences; to proceed mildly, and not with sanguinary prosecutions; and rather to take off the principal authors, by winning and advancing them, than to enrage them by violence and bitterness.

The changes and vicissitude in wars are many: but chiefly in three things; in the seats or stages of the war; in the weapons; and in the manner of the conduct. Wars in ancient time seemed more to move from east to west: for the Persians, Assyrians, Arabians, Tartars, (which were the invaders) were all eastern people. It is true, the Gauls were western; but we read but of two incursions of theirs; the one to Gallo-Graecia, the other to Rome. But east and west have no certain points of heaven: and no more have the wars, either from the east, or west, any certainty of observation. But north and south are fixed: and it hath seldom or never been seen, that the far southern people have invaded the northern, but contrariwise. Whereby it is manifest, that the northern tract of the world is in nature the more martial region: be it in respect of the stars of that hemisphere; or of the great continents that are upon the north, whereas the south part, for ought that is known, is almost all sea; or (which is most apparent) of the cold of the northern parts, which is that which without aid of discipline doth make the bodies hardest, and the courages warmest.

Upon the breaking and shivering of a great state and empire, you may be sure to have wars. For great empires, while they stand, do enervate and destroy the forces of the natives, which they have subdued, resting upon their own protecting forces: and then when they fail also, all goes to ruin, and they become a prey. So was it, in the decay of the Roman empire; and likewise, in the empire of Almaigne, after Charles the Great, every bird taking a feather; and were not unlike to befall to Spain, if it should break. The great accessions and unions of kingdoms do likewise stir up quarrel. For when a state grows to an over-power, it is like a great flood, that will be sure to overflow. As it hath been seen, in the states of Rome, Turkey, Spain, and others. Look when the world hath fewest barbarous peoples, but such as commonly will not marry or generate, except they know means to live (as it is almost everywhere at this day, except Tartary); there is no danger of inundations of people: but when there be great shoals of people, which go on to populate, without foreseeing means of life and sustentation, it is of necessity, that once in an age or two, they discharge a portion of their people upon other nations: which the ancient northern people were wont to do by lot: casting lots, what part should stay at home, and what should seek their fortunes. When a warlike state grows soft and effeminate, they may be sure of a war. For commonly such states are grown rich, in the time of their degenerating; and so the prey inviteth, and their decay in valour encourageth a war.

As for the weapons, it hardly falleth under rule and observation: yet we see, even they have returns and vicissitudes. For certain it is, that ordnance was known in the city of the Oxidrakes in India: and was that, which the Macedonians called thunder and lightning, and magic. And it is well known, that the use of ordnance hath been in China above two thousand years. The conditions of weapons, and their improvement are; first, the fetching a far off: for that outruns the danger: as it is seen in ordnance and muskets. Secondly, the strength of the percussion; wherein likewise ordnance do exceed all arietations, and ancient inventions. The third is, the commodious use of them: as that they may serve in all weathers; that the carriage may be light and manageable; and the like.

For the conduct of the war: at the first, men rested extremely upon number: they did put the wars likewise upon main force, and valour; pointing days for pitched fields, and so trying it out, upon an even match: and they were more ignorant in ranging and arraying their battles. After they grew to rest upon number, rather competent, than vast: they grew to advantages of place, cunning diversions, and the like: and they grew more skilful in the ordering of their battles.

In the youth of a state, arms do flourish: in the middle age of a state, learning; and then both of them together for a time: in the declining age of a state, mechanical arts and merchandise. Learning hath his infancy, when it is but beginning, and almost childish: then his youth, when it is luxuriant and juvenile: then his strength of years, when it is solid and reduced: and lastly, his old age, when it waxeth dry and exhaust. But it is not good, to look too long upon these turning wheels of vicissitude, lest we become giddy. As for the philology of them, that is but a circle of tales, and therefore not fit for this writing.

A Fragment of an Essay of Fame

The poets make fame a monster. They describe her, in part, finely, and elegantly; and, in part, gravely, and sententiously. They say, look how many feathers she hath, so many eyes she hath underneath: so many tongues; so many voices; she pricks up so many ears.

This is a flourish: there follow excellent parables; as that, she gathereth strength in going; that she goeth upon the ground, and yet hideth her head in the clouds. That, in the day time, she sitteth in a watch tower, and flieth most by night: that she mingleth things done, with things not done: and that she is a terror to great cities: but that which passeth all the rest, is: they do recount that the earth, mother of the giants that made war against Jupiter, and were by him destroyed, thereupon, in an anger, brought forth fame: for certain it is, that rebels, figured by the giants, and seditious fames, and libels, are but brothers, and sisters; masculine, and feminine. But now, if a man can tame this matter, and bring her to feed at the hand, and govern her, and with her fly other ravening fowl, and kill them, it is somewhat worth. But we are infected with the style of the poets. To speak now in a sad, and serious manner: there is not, in all the politics, a place less handled, and more worthy to be handled, than this of fame. We will, theretofore, speak of these points. What are false fames; and what are true fames; and how they may be best discerned; how fames may be sown, and raised; how they may be spread, and multiplied; and how they may be checked, and laid dead. And other things, concerning the nature of fame. Fame is of that force, as there is scarcely any great action wherein it hath not a great part; especially, in the war. Mucianus undid Vitellius by a fame that he scattered; that Vitellius had in purpose, to remove the legions of Syria into Germany; and the regions of Germany into Syria: whereupon the legions of Syria were infinitely inflamed. Julius Caesar took Pompey unprovided, and laid asleep his industry, and preparations, by a fame that he cunningly gave out; how Caesar's own soldiers loved him not; and being wearied with the wars, and laden with the spoils of Gaul, would forsake him, as soon as he came into Italy. Livia settled all things, for the succession of her son Tiberius, by continual giving out that her husband Augustus was upon recovery, and amendment. And it is an usual thing, with the bashaws, to conceal the death of the great Turk from the Janissaries, and men of war, to save the sacking of Constantinople, and other towns, as their manner is. Themistocles made Xerxes, king of Persia, post apace out of Graecia, by giving out that the Grecians had a purpose to break his bridge of ships, which he made athwart Hellespont. There be a thousand such like examples; and the more they are, the less they need to be repeated; because a man meeteth with them everywhere: therefore, let all wise governors have as great a watch, and care, over fames, as they have of the actions and designs themselves.

The rest was not finished.

Index of Quotations and Foreign Phrases with Translations

The figures in brackets refer to the pages.

abeunt studia in mores (139) Studies pass into [i.e. go to form] character.

adeste, si (8) Come now, if anything remains for me to do.

amici curiae . . . parasiti curiae (152) friends of the court . . . parasites of the court.

animasque in vulnere (154) and leave their lives ['souls'] in the wound.

at domus (100) But the house of Aeneas shall rule over all the coasts – his children's children, and those that shall be born of them.

atque is habitus (44) The temper of men's minds was such that while only a few dared to do so vile a deed, many desired it and all acquiesced in it.

Caesarem portas (112) You carry Caesar and his fortune.

cogita quam diu (7) Consider how long you have been doing the same things: death may be desired not only by the valiant or the miserable, but also by the victim of ennui.

communia maledicta (155) ill words applicable to all and sundry.

concessum propter duritiem cordis (113) a thing allowed on account of the hardness of men's hearts (*cf.* Matthew xix: 8).

conflata magna invidia (39) When great ill-will has been conceived [towards a ruler], all his acts, good or bad, alike condemn him.

consilium Pompeii (86) Pompey follows a truly Themistoclean policy: he thinks that he who commands the sea, commands all.

cum non sis (30) When you are no longer the man you have been, there is no reason why you should wish to live.

cymini sectores (139) dividers of cummin seed, 'hair-splitters'.

de facto (31) as a fact, as an actual possession.

desemboltura (111) 'dexterity, readiness' (so defined in Richard Percyvall's *Bibliotheca Hispanica,* 1591); adroitness which finds an easy and graceful outlet on all occasions for what it is in a man to do or say.

devita profanas (11) Avoid profane novelties of words and oppositions of science falsely so called (I Timothy vi: 20).

dolendi modus (41) There is a limit to grieving but none to fearing.

duces belli (149) military leaders.

ecce in deserto . . . ecce in penetralibus (9) Behold, he is in the desert . . . behold, he is in the secret chambers (Matthew xxiv: 26).

erant in officio (40) They were full of zeal, and yet rather inclined to discuss than to execute the orders of their officers.

et conversus Deus (31) And God turned to behold the works which his hands had made, and saw that all were very good (Genesis i: 31).

exstinctus amabitur idem (8) The same man [an object of ill-will while alive] shall be loved when his light is out.

faber quisque (111) Every man is the architect of his own fortune.

feri, si (8) Strike, if it be for the good of the Roman people.

fons turbatus (150) A righteous man being cast in his suit in presence of his adversary, is as a troubled fountain and a corrupt spring (Proverbs xxv: 26).

haec pro amicitia (74) These things out of regard for our friendship I have not concealed.

hinc usura vorax (41) Hence usury rapacious, and interest greedily advancing to the reckoning day, hence credit shaken, and war that was a gain to many.

hoc agere (59) keep to the business in hand.

hominem delirum (70) A madman, who wrecks weighty realities on mere verbal subtleties.

idem manebat (117) He remained the same, when it was no longer becoming to him.

ignavum fucos pecus (113) The drones, an idle swarm, they banish from their hives.

illam terra parens (39) Her did mother Earth inflamed with wrath against the Gods, bring forth (so runs the story) youngest sister to Coeus and Enceladus.

ille etiam caecos etc. (39) He also [the sun] often gives warning of dark rebellions imminent, of treachery and hidden warfare brewing.

illi mors gravis (30) Death falls heavy on him who, too well known to all others, dies to himself unknown.

in illo viro (111) There was in him such strength of body and mind that in whatever rank he had been born, he would have been likely to win fortune for himself.

iniquum petas (137) Ask for more than is just, in order to get what is just.

in nocte consilium (59) Night brings counsel.

in studio rei (97) In his pursuit of wealth it was plain that he sought, not food for avarice, but an instrument of doing good .

in sudore vultus alieni (98, 113) in the sweat of another's face.

in sudore vultus tui (112) In the sweat of thy face, shalt thou eat thy bread (Genesis iii: 19).

in veste varietas (10) Let there be variety in the garment, but no rent or cut.

invidia festos (27) Envy keeps no holidays.

ira hominis (12) The wrath of man doth not fulfil the justice of God (James i: 20).

iam Tiberium vires (8) Tiberius was fast losing his bodily strength, but not his gift of dissimulation.

iudicis officium (151) It is a judge's office to inquire not only into the facts of a case, but into the times and occasions thereof.

ius civitatis (83) the right of citizenship; *ius commercii, etc.*: the right of trading, of marriage, of inheritance, of voting, of holding public office.

iuventutem egit (116) He spent a youth full of errors, nay of madnesses.

laudando praecipere (144) to instruct by praising.

legi a se (44) That his soldiers were levied, not bought.

liberatores or *salvatores* (149) deliverers or saviours.

liberius quam (40) More freely than was compatible with respect for their rulers.

Livia, coniugii (8) Farewell, Livia, keep after me the memory of our marriage.

magna civitas (72) A great city is a great solitude.

magnificabo (145) I will magnify mine office (Romans xi: 13).

magno conatu nugas (70) [produce] trifles with great effort.

materiam superabit opus (42) The workmanship will excel the material.

melior natura (46) a better nature.

memento quod es (55) Remember that thou art man – remember that thou art a God, or God's vice-gerent.

mitte ambos (61) Send them both naked before strangers and you shall see.

multum incola fuit (108) My soul hath been a long sojourner (Psalms cxx: 6).

negotiis pares (80, 149) (men who are) equal to conducting affairs.

nomen bonum (144) A good name is like a fragrant ointment. (Ecclesiastes viii: 1)

non deos vulgi (46) It is not profane to deny the gods of the vulgar: but it is profane to apply to the gods the beliefs of the vulgar.

non est curiosus (25) An inquisitive man is sure to be malevolent also.

non est iam dicere (46) We cannot now say: As the people, so is the priest. For in fact the people are not so [bad] as the priest .

non inveniet (58) He shall not find faith on the earth. (Luke xviii: 8) cf. Essay 1, p. 6.

nos scimus (153) We know that the law is good, provided that a man use it lawfully (I Timothy i: 8).

nunc dimittis (8) Now lettest thou [thy servant depart in peace] (Luke ii: 29).

octogesimus octavus (101) eighty-eight, a year of wonders.

omnis fama (148) All reputation comes from those who are of a man's household.

omnium consensu (32) All men deemed him fit for empire – had he never become emperor.

omnium quae dixerat (147) He had an art of displaying to advantage all that he said and did.

optimi consiliarii (58) The best counsellors are the dead.

optimum elige (21) Choose the best, and custom will make it pleasant and easy.

optimus ille (107) He best asserts the soul's freedom, who snaps the fetters that gall his breast, and ceases once for all to suffer.

padre commune (141) common father, father of all alike.

parce, puer (92) Boy, spare the goad, and pull harder at the reins.

participes curarum (73, 149) associates in their cares.

patres patriae (149) fathers of their country.

perpetui principes (148) princes in perpetuity.

per saltum (26) at a bound.

pessimum genus (144) the worst sort of enemies, those that praise you.

Philippis iterum (100) Thou shalt see me again at Philippi.

placebo (59) 'I will please' (Psalms xvi: 9): 'to sing a song of *placebo*' meaning to flatter, to be complaisant.

plenus rimarum sum (57) I am full of chinks.

pluet super eos (151) He shall rain snares upon them (Psalms ix: 6).

poco di matto (111) a little of the fool or madman.

pompa mortis (7) It is the trappings of death that terrify, rather than death itself.

primum mobile (40, 48, 141) 'the first moveable' or 'first moved' (*Paradise Lost* 3, line 483), the tenth sphere or heaven of the old astronomy, which carried round with it in its revolution the lower spheres of the planets and fixed stars.

principis est (58) A prince's greatest virtue is to know his men.

propagatores or *propugnatores imperii* (149) Extenders or defenders of empire.

prudens advertit (63) The wise man takes heed to his own steps: the fool turns aside to deceits (*cf.* Proverbs xiv: 15).

pulchrorum autumnus pulcher (118) The autumn of the beautiful is beautiful.

quam volumus licet (47) Esteem ourselves as we may, senators, yet we are not superior to the Spaniards in numbers, nor to the Gauls in bodily force, nor to the Carthaginians in cunning, nor to the Greeks in arts, nor, indeed, to the Italians and Latins themselves in the inborn domestic sentiment which belongs to this land and nation; but in piety, and religion, and the one great wisdom – the recognition that all is ruled and ordered by the will of the immortal gods – it is here that we have surpassed all tribes and peoples.

quanta patimur (26) How great are our sufferings!

qui de contemnenda (146) Men who write books 'On the duty of despising Glory' allow their name to appear on the title-page.

qui festinat (97) He that maketh haste to be rich shall not be innocent (Proverbs xxviii: 20).

qui finem vitae (8) [A mind] that reckons the close of life one of Nature's boons.

qui fortiter emungit (151) The wringing of the nose bringeth forth blood. (Proverbs xxx: 33).

respondes, altero (70) You reply – with one eyebrow lifted to your forehead and the other drawn down to your chin – that you are no lover of cruelty.

salus populi (152) The people's welfare is the supreme law.

satis magnum (28) We are, one to another, a theatre (or spectacle) ample enough.

secundum genera (58) by classes.

se non diversas (63) He said he did not [like Burrus] cherish hopes from opposite quarters, but looked simply to the Emperor's safety.

serpens nisi serpentem (111) A serpent unless it has eaten a serpent does not become a dragon.

Siete Partidas (149) 'seven parts' (the title of a digest of the laws of Spain).

si vixero (44) If I live, the Roman Empire will have no further need of soldiers.

solus imperantium (32) Vespasian, alone among the emperors, was changed for the better [by empire].

solvam cingula regum (40) I will loose the girdles of kings (Isaiah xlv: 1 *cf.* Job xii: 18).

sospetto licentia fede (91) Suspicion gives faith [*i.e.* fidelity] leave to depart [*i.e.* releases it from all obligation]

species virtutibus similes (144) appearances resembling virtues.

spreta conscientia (144) in disdain of the other's consciousness [of imperfection].

sui amantes (65) Lovers of themselves without a rival.

sunt plerumque (53) The desires of princes are commonly vehement and contradictory one to another.

Sulla nescivit (44) Sulla was ignorant of letters, he could not 'dictate'.

tanquam unus (141) as one of us (Genesis iii: 22).

tantum religio (11) So great the evils to which religion could prompt .

telam honoris crassiorem (155) honour of a coarser web.

terra potens (82) A land mighty in arms and in fertility of soil.

testamenta et orbos (99) Childless men and their bequests were caught by him as in a net.

tu quoque, Galba (100) Thou also, Galba, shalt taste of empire.

ubi peccat (120) Where she errs in the one, she runs a risk in the other.

ultima primis cedebant (117) The last of him was not equal to the first.

ut puto deus fio (8) Meseems I am becoming a God.

vena porta (55, 113) the 'gate-vein' which distributes blood to the liver.

venient annis (100) In later ages there shall come a time, when Ocean shall loose the bands of nature, and a vast continent shall lie open, and Tiphys shall disclose new worlds, and Thule shall no longer be the end of the earth.

ver perpetuum (127) a perpetual Spring.

versatile ingenium (111) versatility.

vetulam suam (23) He preferred his old wife to immortality [i.e. Penelope to Calypso].

vinum daemonum (5) wine of devils.